The Russian Revolution and Its Global Impact

A Short History with Documents

The Russian Revolution and Its Global Impact

A Short History with Documents

Jonathan Daly and Leonid Trofimov

Hackett Publishing Company, Inc.
Indianapolis/Cambridge

20 19 18 17   1 2 3 4 5 6 7

For further information, please address
Hackett Publishing Company, Inc.
P.O. Box 44937
Indianapolis, Indiana 46244-0937

www.hackettpublishing.com

Cover design by Rick Todhunter
Interior design by Laura Clark
Composition by Aptara, Inc.

Library of Congress Cataloging-in-Publication Data
Names: Daly, Jonathan W., author. | Trofimov, Leonid, co-author.
Title: The Russian Revolution and its global impact : a short history with
    documents / Jonathan Daly and Leonid Trofimov.
Description: Indianapolis : Hackett Publishing Company, Inc., 2017. |
    Series: Passages : key moments in history | Includes bibliographical
    references and index.
Identifiers: LCCN 2017007301 | ISBN 9781624666254 (cloth :
    alkaline paper) | ISBN 9781624666247 (paperback : alkaline paper)
Subjects: LCSH: Soviet Union—History—Revolution, 1917–1921. |
    Soviet
    Union—History—Revolution, 1917–1921—Influence. | Soviet
    Union—History—Revolution, 1917–1921—Sources.
Classification: LCC DK265 .D24 2017 | DDC 947.084/1—dc23
LC record available at https://lccn.loc.gov/2017007301

The paper used in this publication meets the minimum requirements of
American National Standard for Information Sciences—Permanence of
Paper for Printed Library Materials, ANSI Z39.48–1984.

∞

For my students, J. D.
For my daughter Maya, L. T.

CONTENTS

PREFACE

Deep in the night of July 16–17, 1918, in the Ural city of Ekaterinburg, secret police (Cheka) officials entered the Ipatiev House, a private home which had been commandeered by the Bolsheviks and made into the maximum-security residence of the former Russian tsar and his family back in April. The two-story stone house was surrounded by a tall wooden stockade and guarded twenty-four hours a day by dozens of security personnel. On July 4, the Cheka had assumed responsibility for guarding the former tsar of all Russia, Nicholas II, and his family.

At around 1:30 a.m., the head of the Ekaterinburg Cheka, Iakov Iurovskii, awakened Nicholas II, Tsarina Alexandra, their five children, three servants, and the court physician Dr. Evgenii Botkin. Having washed and dressed, the eleven were led to the lower level and into a large room with no furniture. Two chairs were brought in at the tsar's request. He sat his hemophiliac son Alexei on one; Alexandra sat on the other. The rest were told to line up. In a few minutes, Iurovskii entered the room with ten armed men. He announced that the local authorities had ordered the tsar and his family shot. The gunmen began shooting immediately, firing dozens of bullets at the hapless victims. Blood splattered everywhere. Some were finished off with bayonets. The lifeless bodies were then carried out to a waiting truck and driven ten miles to the north. There, in the middle of nowhere, the bodies were stripped, burned, and cast into an abandoned mineshaft. The next night, however, Iurovskii took some other men and retrieved the bodies. He had them driven to a more remote site. The men doused the faces and bodies with sulfuric acid and then reburied them.

Operations were also undertaken against the extended family of the tsar. On the night of June 12–13, Bolshevik authorities had arrested his uncle the Grand Duke Michael in the Ural town of Perm, some two hundred miles northwest of Ekaterinburg, and had murdered him. Then, on the night of July 17, outside Alapaevsk, ninety miles north of Ekaterinburg, seven more close relations of Nicholas II were murdered, along with members of their entourage. Most of them were hurled alive down a mineshaft. Clearly, the Bolsheviks wanted to completely wipe out all remnants of the Imperial Romanov dynasty. But why?

The Bolsheviks had seized power in October 1917, in the midst of World War I, after eight months of indecisive rule by shifting coalitions of liberals and socialists who had taken power after the tsar's abdication in early March. The war had gone badly. Social order was breaking down. Economic hardship had intensified. The population craved a new, freer order but also political and economic stability. The Bolsheviks seemed to promise everything the people wanted. They proclaimed an end to the war and negotiated peace in March 1918. They declared an end to private property in land and granted land-starved agricultural laborers the right to work it. An eight-hour day for urban workers was established. National minorities were guaranteed the right to self-determination.

Yet within months all the promises seemed hollow. Factories shut down as owners and managers fled. Many workers protested and voted for opponents of the Bolsheviks who overturned elections and imposed their own activists in the worker councils and trade unions. The treaty with Germany required giving up one-third of European Russia. The grain supply system—already strained from the requirement of feeding millions of troops at the front lines with fewer farmers in the fields—began to break down, as peasants seized and divided up the large estates. In May 1918, the Bolsheviks, desperate to obtain food for the cities, declared "war on the peasant bourgeoisie." Then the 50,000-man Czechoslovak Legion, which was making its way through Siberia to join the fight against German and Austria-Hungary on the Western Front, refused Bolshevik demands that it disarm. The Legion quickly seized control of the Trans-Siberian Railroad from the Volga River to the Pacific Ocean. They reached out to anti-Bolshevik forces, including disgruntled political activists and officers of the old Imperial army, and the Civil War was on. What started out as a popular revolution had turned into a bloody conflict with hostile anti-Bolshevik movements and fronts.

The Civil War was not only a conflict of interests, but also a conflict of visions. The Bolsheviks offered the promise of a world without violence, injustice, inequality, and exploitation while their opponents appealed to the Russians' sense of national pride, honor, and duty, but disagreed among themselves about what should be changed in Russia and what should remain the same. If even one member of the Imperial family—the former tsar, or one of his children, uncles, or cousins—had fallen into the hands of the armed opposition, the Bolshevik leaders presumably reasoned, then he or she could have served as a rallying banner of sacred war against them. The leading Bolsheviks, who were committed to an agenda of destroying and uprooting all traditions, established institutions, and age-old patterns of life, apparently felt they could not risk leaving any of Nicholas's immediate and extended relations at large. At the same time, the Bolsheviks recognized that such actions as murdering in cold blood some two dozen people, including women and children, was unlikely to enjoy the approval of most people in Russia or the wider world. Thus, only the news of the killing of the former tsar was made public at the time. The other deaths were admitted to only in 1926.

With these events in mind, one can argue that the Bolshevik Revolution diverged radically from important earlier revolutions. The English Civil War (1642–1651) pitted parliamentarians against an overreaching monarch and to some extent culminated in 1649 with the beheading of Charles I. Yet this bloody act followed a meticulously conducted public trial and took place in public. England's Glorious Revolution of 1688–1689 involved the deposing of a king but also a carefully articulated set of principles by which the new king was to govern, the Bill of Rights. The American revolutionaries spelled out the reasons for breaking with England in their Declaration of Independence. The French revolutionaries put their king on trial, allowed him a defense attorney, published the judicial proceedings, and executed him in the center of Paris for all to see. What all these revolutionary events had in common was the revolutionaries' desire to justify their actions rationally and in the court of public opinion. By contrast, what the Bolsheviks were engaged in during midsummer 1918 was so beyond the pale of reasonable justification that the full truth about it could not be revealed publicly.

The Bolsheviks adopted dozens of policies that could only be seen as surreal or at least unprecedented in their historical context: the nationalization of all private property; the abolition of the free market; violent campaigns against organized religion; the publication of secret treaties; the repudiation of sovereign debts; the abolition of legal codes and law courts; the legalization of abortion; the radical simplification of divorce; the creation of a worldwide network of subversive political organizations; the formation of a one-party dictatorship; the tight central control of all means of communication and media; the imposition of an official and obligatory artistic doctrine; and the collectivization of agriculture. One could go on and on. Some were proclaimed to the world. Others remained hidden. All had in common a commitment to wipe the slate clean, start from scratch, create a new order, liberate humanity, enact justice, bring to life a new human, and make not just Russia, but eventually the whole world a better place. In sum, the Russian Revolution was a global event with a global agenda.

* * *

Our main goal was to make this book useful not only for those interested in Russian history, but for scholars and students seeking to explore some of the critical dynamics of twentieth-century European and world history. The book was structured with that hope in mind. Both the essay and the documentary sections are divided into three main topics.

The first topic concerns the Russian Revolution itself. It builds on our earlier documentary reader, which comprehensively examined social, political, cultural, and ideological aspects of Russia in the First World War and the revolutionary era.[1] Although the first section of the present book cannot match the scope and depth of our previous volume, it nevertheless aims to provide a detailed introduction to the conditions that led to the Russian Revolution, its main stages, the major political forces and actors, the key events, and the ideas that inspired them. In sum, the first section should give the reader a sufficient understanding of the domestic revolutionary developments in Russia that led to the collapse of the Russian Empire and the birth of Soviet Russia, and of the immediate geopolitical repercussions of these historic events.

The second topic is the unique character of the Soviet approach to international relations and its underlying motivations of revolutionary and state interests. Specific examples of Soviet innovative practices, such as the repudiation of secret treaties and parallel efforts at subversion and diplomacy, are presented along with evidence of the impact of Soviet revolutionary policies on international relations and international security in the 1920s and the 1930s. This topic may be of particular interest to students of twentieth-century international relations.

The third topic has to do with the broader impact of the revolutionary transformation and of "building socialism" in Russia on the hearts and minds of the people around the world. The diverse nature of the

---

1. Jonathan Daly and Leonid Trofimov, eds., *Russia in War and Revolution, 1914–1922: A Documentary History* (Indianapolis, IN: Hackett Publishing Company, 2009).

responses suggests that they were not a mere product of Soviet propaganda, but rather a fusion of communist (or anti-communist) ideas with a wide variety of grievances, fears, and hopes throughout the world. This topic, therefore, could be especially relevant in surveys of major twentieth-century world history themes such as anti-colonialism, fascism, participatory politics, modernization, peace and conflict, and so forth.

Finally, it is not the intent of the authors to present a full and final verdict on the Russian Revolution as a world history phenomenon, but to offer a framework for further discussion and research. We leave it to our readers to develop their own analyses of the historical documents in the book and embark upon a fascinating exploration of events in world history as a shared human experience.

We would like to express our deep gratitude to many people and institutions for support and assistance. We extend many thanks to our editor Rick Todhunter, who first suggested that we pursue this ambitious topic, and his talented and dependable team. We are grateful for financial help from the University of Illinois at Chicago, Bentley University, and Queen's University, which enabled us to conduct research, present our findings at conference venues, commission maps, and secure copyright permissions. We give special thanks to expert cartography by Peter Bull. Research assistance in preparing the maps was supplied by William Briska with most helpful suggestions by Sofya Belova, Dmitry Zhukovsky, Yulia Rubina, and Dmitry Dotsenko. We are grateful to Julia Sergeeva-Albova for her German translation expertise. If this book has any merits, it owes them to a large extent to the insightful, generous, skillful, and expert suggestions and criticism of our colleagues across many fields, including Gleb J. Albert, Sergei Maksudov (Aleksandr Babyonyshev), Richard Levy, Colleen McQuillen, Mark Liechty, Steve Marks, Leon Fink, Junaid Quadri, Joaquín Chavez, Chris Boyer, Marc Stern, Angma Jhala, Sandra Pujals, Bridie Andrews, Sung Choi, and Cyrus Veeser, as well as participants at the Midwest Russian History Workshop in St. Paul, Minnesota, the Pogrankom Interdisciplinary Group in Kingston, Ontario, and the Ninth World Congress of the International Council for East European and Eurasian Studies in Makuhari, Japan.

* * *

Technical Matters

All dates before January 1, 1918, follow the older Julian calendar (O.S.), which was in use in Russia until that date. It lagged thirteen days behind the Gregorian calendar (N.S.) used throughout the Western countries. We observe the Library of Congress transliteration system, minus the diacritical marks, except for widely accepted Latinizations of names, such as Nicholas (not Nikolai) and Trotsky (not Trotskii). Throughout the book, ellipses without spaces (...) are from the original. Unless otherwise specified, all translations are by the authors.

LIST OF MAPS

LIST OF ILLUSTRATIONS

GLOSSARY OF TERMS

African National Congress:
Leading anti-colonialist party of
South Africa founded in 1912

**AMTORG (American Trade
Corporation):** Soviet state trading company in the United States

**ARCOS (All-Russian Co-operative
Society):** Soviet state trading
company in Great Britain

Bloody Sunday: January 9, 1905,
when Imperial troops fired on a
peacefully demonstrating crowd

Bolshevik Party: The founding
and ruling party of the Soviet
Union

Bolsheviks: The more radical and
influential faction of the Russian Social Democratic Party

Central Committee: The most
senior Communist officials that
met in between Party Congresses

Central Powers: Germany,
Austria-Hungary, the Ottoman
Empire, and Bulgaria in World
War I

Cheka: The Extraordinary
Commission, or secret police
(1917–1922)

class: In the Marxist conception,
an immutable socio-economic
category

Comintern: Communist International, a Moscow-based
organization aimed at spreading
revolution

communism: The highest stage of
human development as pre-
dicted by Karl Marx

Communist Party: The name of
the Bolshevik Party from 1918

Constituent Assembly: An
all-Russian political body
democratically elected in late
1917

Duma: The lower chamber of the
parliament created in 1906

GPU: The Main Political
Administration, or secret
police, successor of the Cheka
(1922–1923)

Guomindang: A Chinese nationalist political party founded in
1911

Indian National Congress: The
main pro-independence party in
India, founded in 1885

Kadet: A member of the liberal
Constitutional Democratic
Party

Komsomol: The Communist
Youth League, an arm of the
Bolshevik Party

"kulak": A wealthy peasant. By extension, a rural dweller resisting Bolshevik confiscation of food surpluses and later Stalinist collectivization of agriculture

Marxism: An ideology aimed at abolishing capitalism and attaining socialism and communism

Mensheviks: The more orthodox Marxist faction of the Russian Social Democratic Party

NAACP (National Association for the Advancement of Colored People): An organization for promoting the civil rights of African-Americans founded in 1909

New Economic Policy (NEP): A temporary relaxation of anti-market policies (1921–1928)

October Manifesto: A declaration by Tsar Nicholas II to grant a parliament and civil rights

Octobrist Party: A political party founded to support the October Manifesto

Panslavism: A Russian ideology favoring cooperation and protection of Slavic peoples

Party Congress: A meeting of Communist Party officials convened to make major decisions

peasant: A traditional farmer and a member of a rural community

People's Commissariat: Main government department or ministry

Petrograd Soviet: The worker and soldier council of Petrograd

Politburo: The top Communist Party governing body

Populists: Radical intellectuals seeking to liberate the Russian peasant masses through revolution

Pravda: The flagship newspaper of the Soviet Communist Party

proletarian: An industrial worker

proletariat: The class of industrial workers

The Red Scare: Political reaction to the Bolshevik Revolution in the United States

Reds: The Bolsheviks or Communists

Russian Social Democratic Party: The principal Marxist party of Russia

serf: A peasant tied to the land until emancipation in 1861

socialism: An ideology emphasizing social justice, common ownership of property, and collective production of wealth

Socialist-Revolutionary Party: Party with aim to liberate Russian people via revolution and terrorism

Soviet: A council or form of local self-government beginning in 1917 soon coopted by Bolsheviks

Soviet power: The Bolshevik term for their rule and their regime

Sovnarkom: The Council of People's Commissars, or the Soviet government

speculation: The act of engaging in market relations; prohibited by the Bolsheviks

SRs: Members of the Socialist-Revolutionary Party

Treaty of Brest-Litovsk: A treaty that ended war between Russia and the Central Powers in 1918

tsar: The monarch of Russia

USSR: The Union of Soviet Socialist Republics or Soviet Union

Versailles Conference: A meeting outside Paris in 1919–1920 to decide peace terms

Versailles Treaty: The document that formally ended war between the Allies and Germany in 1919

War Communism: Radical economic policies pursued by the Bolsheviks during the Civil War

Whites: Anti-Bolshevik forces during the Russian Civil War

Zemstvo(s): Institution(s) of local self-government created in 1864

CHRONOLOGY OF WAR AND REVOLUTION

1905
9 January: Bloody Sunday rally and shooting in Saint Petersburg
5 September: The Russian-Japanese War ends with Russia's defeat
17 October: Tsar's Manifesto promises civil liberties and a parliament

1910
Mexican Revolution begins
Republican revolution in Portugal

1911
Chinese Revolution begins

1912
8 January: South African Native National Congress founded (renamed African National Congress in 1923)

1914
June–July: Mass strikes in St. Petersburg
15/28 July: Austria-Hungary declares war on Serbia
17/30 July: Russian order for general mobilization
19 July/1 August: German declaration of war on Russia

1915
Military supply crisis (insufficiency of shells and/or equipment)
March: France and Britain promise Russia control over Constantinople after war
26 August: Nicholas assumes supreme military command against advice of his ministers

1916

Gradual disorganization of railroad system; grave fuel and food shortages; massive inflation

22 May/4 June: Brusilov Offensive begins, dealing powerful blow to Austria-Hungary

17 December: Rasputin is murdered

1917

23 February: Spontaneous demonstrations in Petrograd caused by bread shortage in stores

27 February: Petrograd declared in state of siege; mass troop mutiny in Petrograd

March: Formation of soviets in cities, factories, military units, and countryside

1 March: Order Number 1 abolishes military chain of command

2 March: Provisional Government formed; Nicholas abdicates

9 March: The United States recognizes Provisional Government

4 April: Lenin's "April Theses" call for a deepening of revolution

18 June–5 July: Failed offensive against Austria-Hungary; troops mutiny

25–31 August: Alleged mutiny by Kornilov (Kornilov Affair)

25–26 October (night): Bolshevik-dominated Congress of Soviets passes decrees on peace and land

Late October–November: Soviet power spreads across country and through military units

12 November: Elections to Constituent Assembly begin

17 November: Nationalization of private enterprise

22 November: Decree on elective courts and revolutionary tribunals

23 November: Finland declares independence from Russia

28 November: Kadets proclaimed "enemies of people"

7 December: Extraordinary Commission to Fight Counterrevolution and Sabotage (Cheka) set up

9 December: Brest-Litovsk peace talks begin

10 December: Formation of coalition government of Bolsheviks and Left SRs

14 December: Nationalization of banks

18 December: Decree on civil marriage; Sovnarkom recognizes independence of Finland

1918

2 January: Decrees on "laborers' rights" and on universal labor obligation

5–6 January: Constituent Assembly opens and shut down at gun point

11 January: Ukrainian Central Rada proclaims Ukraine independence

15 January: Sovnarkom decrees establishment of Red Army

20 January: Separation of church and state proclaimed

21 January: Repudiation of all Russian state debts

25 January: The Ukrainian People's Republic proclaims independence

27 January: Ukraine signs peace treaty with Central Powers

1 February (N.S.): Gregorian calendar instituted (Julian dates February 1–13 dropped)

18 February: Germany and Austria-Hungary abrogate truce and begin broad offensive against Russia

3 March: Treaty of Brest-Litovsk signed

8 March: Bolshevik party renamed Russian Communist Party

10–12 March: Government moves to Moscow

27 March: Uprising of Don Cossacks against Bolsheviks

5 April: Allied military intervention begins

13 April: Kornilov killed by stray shell; Denikin assumes command of Volunteer Army

22 April: Foreign trade nationalized; establishment of universal military training

13 May: Beginning of "War Communism"

25–26 May: Czechoslovak Legion (50,000 soldiers) refuses Bolshevik order to disarm

28 May: Martial law instituted across country

29 May: Universal military draft

8 June: Czechs occupy Samara

12–13 June: Murder of Grand Duke Michael in Perm

28 June: Nationalization of all heavy industry, mining, and railroads

July–August: Numerous peasant revolts

16–17 July: Execution of Imperial family in Ekaterinburg

17 July: Murder at Alapaevsk of several grand dukes and their companions

23 July: Volunteer Army takes Stavropol and by December entire Kuban region

25 July–August: Czechs take Ekaterinburg, Simbirsk, Ufa, Kazan, Irkutsk, and Chita

2 August: Allies occupy Archangelsk

30 August: SR terrorists kill Petrograd Cheka head Uritskii, wound Lenin

2 September: Decree declaring country a single military camp

11 November: Armistice ends World War I

11 November: Poland declares restoration of sovereignty

13 November: Annulment of Treaty of Brest-Litovsk; Red Army begins occupation of Ukraine, Belorussia, and Baltic region

21 November: Ban on all retail and wholesale commerce

10 December: Labor Code establishes universal labor obligation, ages 16–50

1919

18 January: 1919 Paris Peace Conference opens in Versailles

6 February: General strike breaks out in Seattle

8 February: Congress on defense of childhood declares family "dying institution"

2–6 March: First Congress of Comintern, Communist International

6 April: Bavarian Soviet Republic proclaimed

21 March: Hungarian Soviet Republic proclaimed

April: Red Scare begins in the United States

3 May: Bavarian Soviet Republic falls

July: Red Army takes Ekaterinburg, Cheliabinsk, Perm, and Kungur

1 August: Hungarian Soviet Republic falls

13 October: Denikin forces seize Orel, threatening Moscow

16 October: Iudenich nears Petrograd

20 October: Red Army retakes Orel

21–24 October: Red Army repulses Iudenich and captures Tobol'sk and Voronezh

19 November: General offensive of Red Army begins in the south and southeast

1920

30 January: Allies decide to evacuate their forces from Far East

February: Red Army takes Kiev, Poltava, and all Right-Bank Ukraine

4 February: Massive anti-Bolshevik peasant uprising breaks out in Volga region

25 February: General retreat of Volunteer Army commences

29 March–5 April: Party Congress votes to abolish private property and militarize economy

24 April: Poland begins anti-Soviet offensive; Soviet-Polish War begins

12 June: Red Army retakes Kiev

July–September: Peasant uprising in Saratov province

8 July: The United States lifts trade embargo on Soviet Russia

21 July–6 August: Second Congress of Comintern

August: Tambov Uprising begins

October: Soviet All-Russian Co-operative Society (ARCOS) established to conduct trade with Britain

12 October: Peace treaty signed with Poland, ceding portions of Ukraine and Belorussia

14 October: Peace treaty signed with Finland

14 November: Vrangel's forces evacuate Crimea and retreat to Turkey

18 November: Abortion legalized

28 November: The Communist University of the National Minorities of the West established

1921
25–27 February: Red Army invades Georgia and establishes Georgian SSR
28 February–11 March: Strikes in Petrograd
28 February–18 March: Kronstadt sailors rebel "for soviets without Communists"
March: Kronstadt Rebellion
8–16 March: Tenth Party Congress proclaims New Economic Policy (NEP); ban on party factions
16 March: Anglo-Soviet Trade Agreement
21 April: The Communist University of the Toilers of the East established
Summer: Famine begins in Volga region and southern Ukraine (1.5–2 million die through 1922)
23–31 July: The Communist Party of China founded

1922
10 April–19 May: International conference in Genoa
16 April: German-Soviet Treaty on economic and military cooperation signed in Rapallo
Fall: Expulsion of 160 scholars, philosophers, professors—flower of Russia's intelligentsia
30 December: First Congress of Soviets of USSR affirms Treaty on Formation of USSR

1923
January: French and Belgian troops enter the Ruhr region
September–October: Revolutionary movement in Hamburg, Saxony, and Thuringia
November: Adolf Hitler jailed after failed Munich putsch and begins writing *Mein Kampf*

1924
21 January: Lenin dies
2 February: Britain recognizes USSR
27 May: Soviet American Trading Corporation (AMTORG) established to conduct trade with United States
24 October: "Zinoviev letter" published in the British press

1925

March–April: Stalin proclaims "Socialism in One Country"
12 April: Slaughter of Chinese Communists in Shanghai
September: Sun Yat-sen University established
30 October: France recognizes USSR

1926

May: International Lenin School established
3–13 May: General strike in Britain

1927

10 February: Comintern-sponsored League against Imperialism established in
  Brussels
May: ARCOS offices raided by British police, British diplomatic relations with
  USSR severed
October: Tenth anniversary of October Revolution international celebration in
  Moscow
December: Failed Canton uprising in China

1929

February: Trotsky expelled from USSR
3 October: Diplomatic relations restored with UK
21 December: Fiftieth birthday of Stalin; start of cult of personality
27 December: Stalin announces universal collectivization and "liquidation of
  kulaks as class"

1930

26 June–3 July: Sixteenth Party Congress confirms rapid industrialization

1932

31 December: Five-Year Plan proclaimed completed in four years

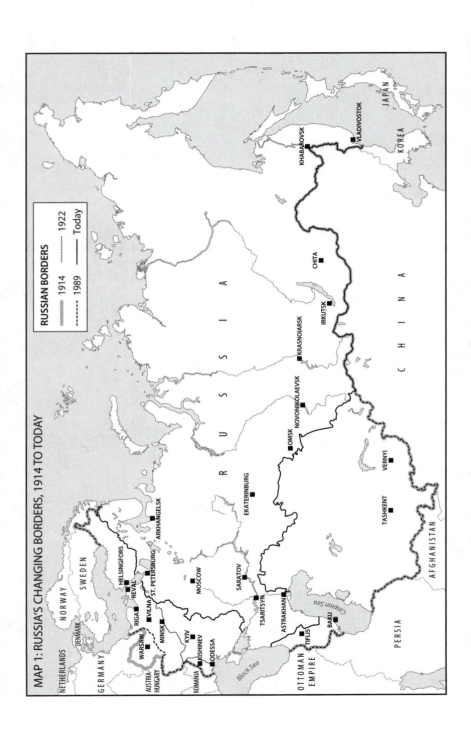

MAP 1: RUSSIA'S CHANGING BORDERS, 1914 TO TODAY

HISTORICAL ESSAY

Russia in Revolution and Civil War

Even after the collapse of the Soviet Union in 1991 and the consequent loss of one-third of its territory, Russia remains the world's largest country on earth (see Map 1). It comprises one-sixth of the earth's landmass stretching across eleven time zones and drains into five of the world's seventeen longest rivers (the Yenisei, Ob', Lena, Amur, and Volga). No country boasts more natural resources. Few developed countries are so ethnically diverse (see Map 2). Although Russians constitute just over 80 percent of the population, more than one hundred ethnic minorities call Russia home. For the most part they now live in peace, but tensions among national minorities contributed to the collapse of both the Imperial and the Soviet states. This turmoil resulted in the creation of seventeen independent countries.[1]

The first (and only) general census of the Russian Empire counted 125.6 million people in 1897, with just under 17 million (13.4 percent) in cities and the rest spread over the countryside. The population grew roughly 200 percent in the nineteenth century and some 30 percent from 1900 to 1914, adding more than two million per year on the eve of the Great War, faster than any major European country. Indeed, Germany entered World War I partly out of fear of Russian population (and industrial) growth. Yet infant mortality was also the highest in Europe: in 1910, of 1,000 children 271 died before turning one, compared to 111 in France.[2] Most Russian peasants remained semiliterate and lived in extended families. Unlike American farmers or French peasants, most Russian peasants did not individually own their

---

1. Finland, Poland, Lithuania, Latvia, Estonia, Russia, Ukraine, Belarus, Moldova, Georgia, Armenia, Azerbaijan, Kazakhstan, Kyrgyzstan, Tajikistan, Turkmenistan, and Uzbekistan.

2. B. R. Mitchell, *European Historical Statistics, 1750–1970* (New York: Columbia University Press, 1978), 42–43.

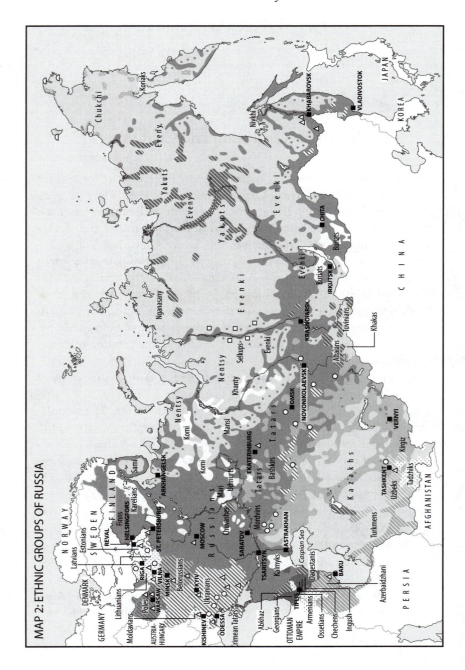

MAP 2: ETHNIC GROUPS OF RUSSIA

SLAVIC PEOPLES

Russians

Ukrainians

Belorussians

Poles

OTHER INDO-EUROPEAN PEOPLES

Armenians, Latvians, Lithuanians, Moldavians, Ossetians, Tadzhiks

○ Germans

△ Jews

TURKIC PEOPLES

Bashkirs, Kazakhs, Kirgiz, Tatars

Uzbeks

Azerbaidzhani, Turkmen

Other Turkic peoples

OTHER URALIC AND ALTAIC PEOPLES

Altaians, Buriats, Estonians, Evenki, Eveny, Finns, Kalmyks, Karelians, Khanty, Komi, Mansi, Mari, Mordvins, Nentsy, Nganasany, Sami, Selkups, Udmurts

CAUCASUS PEOPLES

Abkhaz, Chechens, Dagestanis, Georgians, Ingush

PALEO-SIBERIAN PEOPLES

Chukchi, Koriaks, Nivkhi

◁ Eskimos

▫ Kets

Uninhabited or sparsely settled

Drawn on the basis of *Geograficheckii atlas SSSR dlia srednei shkoly* (Moscow: Glavnoe Upravlenie Geodezii i Kartografi pri SNK SSSR, 1941). Source: Wikimedia Commons.

Figure 1: Sergei Prokudin-Gorskii,
Russian Peasants during Harvest
Time (1909)

Figure 2: Sergei Prokudin-Gorskii,
Bridge over the Kama River on the
Trans-Siberian Railroad (ca. 1910)

land, which belonged to the rural communes of which they were members. Many such communes, especially in the central provinces, suffered
from "land hunger": land allotments grew smaller and the price of land
increased (doubling in 1860–1905), yet yields barely rose, forcing millions to supplement their incomes with non-agricultural work. While
relatively small, in the second half of the nineteenth century the urban
population of the Empire was growing rapidly (from 6 percent in 1861
to 18 percent in 1913), and so were the ranks of industrial workers.
Most worked eleven and a half hours a day (the standard set by a law
of 1897), lived in unsanitary and cramped barracks attached to their
places of work, constantly put their health at risk, and suffered indig-
nities and abuse from foremen and other authorities. Many retained
close ties with their former rural communities and were not fully at
home in either the city or the countryside. It could be argued that the
Russian Empire entered the twentieth century afflicted by the worst of
two worlds (see Figures 1 and 2): the world of tradition that shaped
Russian peasants' antiquated attitudes and practices and the world of
industrial modernization, which brought about not only technological
breakthroughs and expanding literacy but also social dislocation and
economic exploitation. While most peasants continued to farm with
methods and tools abandoned in western Europe hundreds of years
before, the Trans-Siberian Railroad—one of the world's greatest feats
of engineering and industrialization at that time—linked the Empire's
central provinces, Siberia, and the Pacific coast.

Figure 3: Aleksandr Makovsky,
Portrait of Nicholas II of Russia
in his coronation robe (1896)

The country's government and leadership were antiquated as well. When filling out his census questionnaire, Nicholas II of the Romanov dynasty, tsar (ruler) of Russia (see Figure 3), stated as his occupation: "Master [*khoziain*] of the Russian Land." Nicholas believed that autocracy, the most extreme form of absolutist monarchy, allowed him to rise above corruption, intrigue, and selfishness and to focus on what was best for the Russian land and its people overall. A shared Orthodox Christian faith, he imagined, imbued his subjects with a sense of love, community, and belonging that no secular democracy or republic could hope to achieve. Instead of relishing his autocratic power, however, Nicholas viewed it as a burden and a sacred legacy to be preserved and passed intact to his son. Nicholas's tutor Konstantin Pobedonostsev helped cultivate these views (see Document 1.1). Nicholas was also steadfastly supported in this outlook by his German-born and British-raised wife, Alexandra, a granddaughter of Queen Victoria and a devout convert to the Orthodox Christian faith.

Most of the country's educated elites rejected these views. For them, Russia needed to continue its efforts to emulate Western European countries. This trajectory had begun when Peter the Great (r. 1682–1725) built up a European-style military, bureaucracy, diplomatic corps, capital city, and educational institutions. He also sent many hundreds of young men to Europe to study.

Most of Peter's successors carried forward this work. Most importantly, the grandfather of Nicholas II, Alexander II (r. 1855–1881), abolished serfdom (an institution that legally bound peasants to land owned by gentry), founded institutions of local self-government (the Zemstvos and the town councils), and created an independent judiciary, with trial by jury and an autonomous bar. These wide-ranging and profound changes came to be known as "the Great Reforms." For Russian radicals (many of them young, with some university education) this was not good enough. To them, nothing short of the complete overthrow of the Imperial regime could lift the burden of economic and political oppression and liberate the Russian people. Many dreamed of socialism—a radically different vision of economic and social organization based on the principles of collective production of wealth, and social and political equality. These radicals who often called themselves Populists, claimed to speak on the behalf of "the People" and tried to stir up the Russian peasants. When that failed, they turned to political terrorism, killing several government officials and staging six failed attempts on the life of Alexander II. The seventh assassination attempt, in March 1881, was successful. It occurred at the very moment when Alexander had finally agreed to create a national consultative assembly. Nicholas, who was thirteen at the time, watched in horror as his grandfather, who had brought to life major reforms, screamed and died in agony in the Winter Palace, following the bomb attack.

In response, Nicholas's father, Alexander III (r. 1881–1894), crushed the revolutionary opposition and sought to reverse some of the Great Reforms. Access for women and ethnic minorities to secondary and higher education was restricted. Alexander III supported the gentry, which owned a vastly disproportionate, albeit declining, share of arable land, and vigorously pursued Russification in the Empire's western provinces. Printed publications in Ukrainian were forbidden, Russian became the main language of instruction in Poland, and Jews continued to be confined to the Pale of Settlement—specifically designated areas in western provinces they could not leave. In 1891 thousands of Jewish artisans were expelled from Moscow. At the same time, Alexander III enthusiastically promoted industrialization, which placed increased fiscal burden on the peasants and expanded the number of factory workers. To the Russian professional middle classes, the implicit message was clear: make money and forget about politics. Eager to promote industrial modernization, Alexander III and his government adopted some fairly liberal factory legislation but failed to serve as impartial arbiters in the growing number of conflicts between industrialists and the labor force. When Nicholas came to the throne, he affirmed his commitment to autocracy—to the bitter disappointment of those in the educated classes who had hoped that the young tsar and his English-speaking wife would move towards constitutionalism. Ongoing popular unrest would force Nicholas's hand.

Massive strikes by textile workers broke out in 1896 and 1897. Even when workers pursued economic demands, government prohibition of strikes, not to mention unionized activity, helped politicize worker unrest. As the worker ranks and unrest grew, so did the appeal of Marxism, a theory and vision of socialism developed by Karl Marx (1818–1883). Marx emphasized the role of industrial workers (proletarians), predicting they would overthrow the capitalist order and establish socialism and eventually communism, which he conceived as the pinnacle of human progress, development, and liberation from oppression of all kinds. Marxist Social-Democratic parties had flourished in western Europe. Now it was Russia's turn.

Born into the family of a provincial school inspector, Vladimir Lenin (see Figure 4), born Ulyanov (1870–1924), excelled in high school and in law at Kazan University. He had good prospects of joining the growing ranks of the Russian professional middle class. Apolitical during his teenage years, Vladimir was devastated when in 1887 his older brother Alexander was hanged for a failed attempt to kill the tsar. Having devoured his brother's populist books and articles, which he previously had scorned, Vladimir was slowly drawn to the apparent scientific clarity and certainty of Marxism. He began engaging in anti-government activity first in Kazan and then in Saint Petersburg. In 1898, he and other representatives of various small Social-Democratic groups joined together to create the loosely structured Russian Social-Democratic Worker Party.

Lenin's intellectual and organizational leadership skills quickly pushed him to the top of the party. Five years later, the party split over questions of organization and, eventually, tactics into two wings: the Lenin-led Bolsheviks (the majoritarians) and the Mensheviks (the minoritarians), led by Julius Martov (1873–1923; see Figure 4). Over time, the Bolsheviks and the Mensheviks diverged sharply, as the former advocated a more rigid, centralist, and secretive party model and stressed the primacy of political goals over the economic concerns of labor.

In 1899, university students protested across the country. Such protests would occur with great frequency. Political terrorism struck again in 1901—with the assassination of the minister of education—and again and again over the following years. In 1902, major agrarian unrest broke out in the South. Also in 1902, the biggest revolutionary party, the Socialist-Revolutionaries (SRs), was founded. Their leaders, including Viktor Chernov (1873–1952), Ekaterina Breshko-Breshkovskaia (1844–1934), and Grigorii Gershuni (1870–1908) primarily championed the needs of

Figure 4: Lenin (center, seated), Martov (right, seated),
and other members of an early Social-Democratic
organization (1897)

the Russian peasantry. They agitated for popular action, dreamed of a popular revolution, and staged bold terrorist attacks against top government officials in the hope of triggering one. Also in 1902, liberals in exile abroad led by Peter Struve (1870–1944) began publishing a newspaper, *Liberation*, calling for the establishment of a constitutional order. In early 1904, Struve and other leading intellectuals formed an underground Union of Liberation to pursue these goals.

Throughout these years, despite numerous challenges at home, Nicholas II had been pursuing an expansionist policy in the Far East. He viewed Japan, Russia's chief imperial competitor in far northeastern China and Korea, as dramatically inferior to the Europeanized Russians with their immense resources and huge population. In February 1904, however, the Japanese carried out a surprise attack against the Russian Eastern Fleet in Port Arthur, which Russia had leased from China. Over the course of the next year and a half, Russia suffered defeat after defeat on sea and on land. The proponents of constitutionalism began to see the autocratic regime as incapable of carrying out fundamental tasks of state.

On January 9, 1905, multitudes of industrial workers of Saint Petersburg led by a radical priest Grigorii Gapon (1870–1906), took to the streets, many with their family members, to deliver to Nicholas a petition containing complaints of poor living and working conditions and demands for an eight-hour work day, civil rights, and political representation. "If you do not respond to our pleading," it stated, "we will die right here on this square, right before your palace. We do not have anywhere to go and no reason to. We have only two paths: either to freedom and happiness, or to the grave." The tsar was away, but his troops fired at the crowds, killing dozens of people. This day came to be known as "Bloody Sunday" and marked the beginning of the first Russian Revolution. Turmoil continued for months as workers went on strike, peasants attacked gentry estates, and terrorists killed and wounded hundreds of government officials. Whatever their disagreements, the opponents of the regime were willing to overlook them for the sake of the common cause. In the fall, amid a general strike—which all but shut down the economy—Nicholas II reluctantly issued his "October Manifesto," which promised to establish a parliament and basic civil liberties. These promises were enshrined in the Fundamental Laws of April 1906, including a bicameral legislature, with a popularly elected lower chamber, the Duma, and a largely appointed upper chamber, the State Council.

It has been debated to what extent the new political system limited Nicholas's power and whether it was stable and sustainable. Nicholas II remained the Supreme Commander of the Russian armed forces and retained the authority to appoint ministers, provincial governors, and other senior officials. He could dissolve the Duma and call for new elections at will. In 1907, he illegally altered the electoral law to restrict democratic representation. He also maintained control over the secret police and the bureaucracy. Yet the Fundamental Laws gave the parliament real legislative powers, allowed for the creation of oppositional political parties and groups, such as the Constitutional Democratic Party (the Kadets) led by Pavel Miliukov (1859–1943), which called for a full transition to constitutional parliamentarism, and the more moderate Octobrist Party led by Aleksandr Guchkov (1862–1936), which was critical of the government, but pleased with the terms of the October Manifesto. Certain legal protections extended even to Bolshevik and SR activists, some of whom became Duma deputies, and to their publications, which could only be permanently closed down by the courts. Perhaps most important in the long run, the Fundamental Laws made possible the development of a vibrant Russian public sphere, which included trade unions, professional and business organizations, charitable groups, thousands of other voluntary associations, a lively periodical press, and so forth.

Some government officials, including Prime Minister Stolypin (1862–1911), embraced the new political realities. Stolypin was known for his efforts to modernize the Russian countryside by encouraging individual farming and peasant resettlement from those areas where the shortage of land was most dire. He did not shy away from confronting his revolutionary opponents in the Duma with phrases like "These gentlemen want great cataclysms, we want a great Russia." The opposition had its own share of jabs, charging him with brutal suppression of the revolutionary unrest and referring to hangmen's nooses as "Stolypin neckties." Nicholas, for his part, increasingly distanced himself from Stolypin. He considered the entire new constitutional arrangement an aberration, extorted from him under duress when his troops were tied up in Manchuria and exploited by radicals seeking to organize the next revolution. When Stolypin proposed to lift some of the many restrictions on Jews, most of whom were confined to residence in the Pale of Settlement, Nicholas refused, asserting that his "conscience" did not allow it.

By 1909, the major revolutionary parties had fallen on hard times. They lost membership, in part thanks to Russia's booming economic growth, and suffered continuous police repression. But politically and socially, Russia was far from stable. Stolypin was assassinated in 1911 by a revolutionary activist and one-time police informant. The bloody massacre of hundreds of mineworkers in a Siberian gold field in April 1912, who had been protesting their working conditions, set off a strike movement and breathed new life into the labor movement. Intermittent strikes continued for the next two years culminating in the Petrograd general strike in the summer of 1914, which pursued economic as well as political demands.

On June 28, 1914, Archduke Franz Ferdinand, heir to the Austro-Hungarian throne was assassinated in Bosnia by a group of terrorists with ties to a Serbian government. On July 28, Austria-Hungary declared war on Serbia, a Slavic Orthodox Christian country with links to Russia. Nicholas felt compelled politically and diplomatically to order the mobilization of the Russian army to defend Serbia against Austria-Hungary. On September 1, Austria-Hungary's staunchest ally, Germany, declared war on Russia in response to a general mobilization of the Russian army and immediately attacked France, which had been bound by a treaty to defend Russia. Two days later Britain jumped in to protect France and Belgium, and the Great War, later called World War I, had begun. Aside from pursuing Panslavic solidarity, Nicholas and his advisors hoped to reassert Russia's power in the Balkans.

For a while Russian society, political parties, and the tsar seemed united by a shared desire to fight and win the war. Nicholas met with Duma deputies and appeared on the balcony of his Winter Palace to cheering crowds, not far from where nine years earlier his troops had shot workers on Bloody Sunday. A very different kind of violence occurred in May 1915, as crowds in Moscow looted hundreds of businesses and residences they took to be owned by Germans.

Conservatives, liberals, and even many Socialist-Revolutionaries and Social Democrats believed that Russia's cause was just. Lenin and his supporters remained bitterly opposed. To Lenin the war was "a war of plunder," a sign of irreconcilable contradictions within capitalism. As the war unfolded, Lenin found refuge in Switzerland. In September 1915, he attended a socialist conference in Zimmerwald, where he advocated turning the "imperialist war" into a "civil war" to advance socialism. His failure convinced him that the "Second International" (an international association of socialist parties) no longer served the interests of the working class. While in Switzerland, Lenin attempted a major Marxist re-evaluation of capitalism. He recognized that in almost seventy years since the publication of Marx's *Communist Manifesto*, capitalism had spread across countries and continents, along with Europe's colonial empires. Lenin therefore sought to adapt Marx's analysis of capitalism to these realities. He built on earlier efforts to reexamine capitalism by John A. Hobson (1858–1940), Rudolf Hilferding (1877–1941), and Karl Kautsky (1854–1938), but went further, arguing that imperialism—a global system of financial exploitation and domination—was not just a phase, but the final phase of capitalism's development. Lenin further claimed that imperialist capitalism engendered the rise of monopolistic corporate structures that worked to divide and re-divide the world. In other words, capitalism as a free-market system was dying out, making way for—in fact, laying the foundation for—a more efficient and pro-ductive form of economic development based on conscious planning (see Document 1.2).

The implications of this view for the Russian Revolution were immense. However underdeveloped, the Russian Empire was part of this global imperialist system. Its collapse could be achieved in conjunction with the

Figure 5: Lenin in 1920

collapse of imperialism all over the world and perhaps could even contribute to this collapse. Therefore, Lenin (see Figure 5) and his supporters in the Bolshevik Party saw the Russian Revolution as part of a global revolutionary transformation and expected it to address not just Russian, but global inequities.

The Great War was a revolution in itself, for Europe as a whole, and for Russian society in particular. Russia's crushing defeat in the Russo-Japanese War paled in comparison to the impact of mass mobilizations, economic disruptions, material devastation, and demographic catastrophe of this conflict. Most horrifying, the country suffered nearly ten million casualties (military dead, wounded, captured, and missing in action) during the war. Russia's initial incursion into East Prussia resulted in catastrophic defeat at the Battle of Tannenberg and the encirclement of its 2nd Army, whose commander, General Aleksandr Samsonov (1859–1914), committed suicide. By late September 1915, the Germans controlled all of Russian Poland and Lithuania and much of Latvia. The Russian Empire lost jurisdiction over twenty-three million of its subjects, and the people of Poland, the Baltic regions, and eventually Ukraine learned to navigate in a new reality in which the German, the Austro-Hungarian, and the Russian Empires continued to fight for influence and power. Equally important, the strains of total war shattered the traditional worldview of Russia's peasants, who made up nearly the entire Russian Imperial army. As the war dragged on, keeping the soldiers thousands of miles from home, nothing seemed steady or certain anymore: neither the norms of social hierarchy, nor the wisdom and goodness of the tsar, nor the existence of divine providence (see Document 1.3).

In 1915, as the Russian army retreated and munitions shortages intensified, even political moderates and nationalists began to accuse the government of gross incompetence or worse. Relations between the

Duma and senior officials, who remained accountable to the tsar only, were dysfunctional. Nicholas had to dismiss War Minister Vladimir Sukhomlinov (1848–1926) amidst charges of malfeasance and corruption. In late summer 1915, moderate opposition parties in the Duma formed the "Progressive Bloc" to demand further change in government. Critical voices could be heard in the press, in military-industrial committees, which had been set up to facilitate collaboration between government and business, and in the recently formed Association of the Town Councils and the Zemstvos.

Implicitly and sometimes explicitly, critics blamed Nicholas who only made himself more vulnerable when he took on the role of commander-in-chief in September 1915, thus assuming responsibility for both victory and defeat. Indeed, both the military and economic situation continued to deteriorate. A strike movement gained momentum from late 1915, the transportation system was overstrained, inflation raged, and the government lost public support. Even the politically moderate Constitutional Democrat Vasilii Maklakov (1869–1957) felt compelled to call Nicholas a "mad driver" at the helm of Russia.

In 1916 the situation turned from bad to worse as general Aleksei Brusilov's initially successful counteroffensive against Austria-Hungary ran out of steam, adding half a million to Russia's rising casualty toll, while the government's attempts to conscript the empire's subjects in Central Asia to serve in labor battalions on the Eastern Front led to an open rebellion by the Kazakh and Kyrgyz peoples. On November 1, 1916, the Constitutional Democratic leader Miliukov attacked the government in a passionate speech, which included the open-ended refrain: "Is it stupidity or is it treason?" He even mentioned Empress Alexandra, implying approval of (false but widespread) rumors that she was a German spy. With Nicholas at General Headquarters near the frontlines, Alexandra took more interest in matters of state and government appointments. Deeply religious and eager to boost Nicholas's power and to alleviate the suffering of their hemophilic son Aleksei, Aleksandra had turned to "a man of God," a Siberian peasant with hypnotic abilities, Grigorii Rasputin (1869–1916). In their correspondence, the Imperial couple referred to him as a most trusted "Friend." With Nicholas often absent from Petrograd (Saint Petersburg, which sounded too German, was renamed in September 1914), Rasputin recommended for high office his political favorites, and Alexandra passed his recommendations along to the tsar, who sometimes adopted them. Such interventions seemed suspicious and, along with rumors that Rasputin was the tsarina's lover and a German spy to boot, undoubtedly harmed the prestige of the dynasty. In mid-December 1916, he was murdered by two devout monarchists anxious to save it.

As the Russian Empire entered its last months of existence, organized revolutionary activity in Russia's capital remained subdued. The Imperial government had successfully disrupted the leading revolutionary parties—in particular the SRs and the Bolsheviks—by arresting activists. But these successes offered false comfort. The prestige of the dynasty and the government hit an all-time low. Horrific suffering on the front lines; stricter discipline in the factories; labor shortages, rising inflation, and the declining value of the ruble; tighter censorship; continuous military reversals; shortages of fuel and bread; and rumors of more shortages often made life miserable. All the strands of disgruntlement came together in early 1917.

The winter of 1916–1917 was harsh: extreme cold combined with excessive snowfall. Insufficiency of fuel and bread further worsened living conditions in Petrograd. Strikes broke out on January 9 to commemorate the anniversary of Bloody Sunday. Arrests followed, but the strikes continued. On February 22, when the temperature shot up to a balmy 46°F, thousands took to the streets, but government officials believed they had the situation under control. On that very day Nicholas returned to General Headquarters.

For Ilia Gordienko (1884–1957), a Bolshevik activist in the Vyborg district of Petrograd, the revolution, or "the February Days," as they were called later, began on February 23. It was International Women's Day, a holiday that had originated in the United States in 1909 and was celebrated by socialist activists internationally before and during the war. Gordienko recalled hearing female shouts coming from a nearby factory: "Stop working! Come out!" and "Down with the war! Down with high prices! Down with hunger! Bread to workers!" The number of striking workers grew by the day (see Map 3). Students and city residents, including many women protesting food shortages, joined them. Nicholas had no idea how serious the unrest was, since his top officials did not want to worry him. He gave orders to disperse the crowds with military force. Now the critical question was whether the soldiers of the Petrograd garrison could be relied upon to carry out the order. Many were older reservists, deeply unhappy to be drafted at an advanced age. Mass shootings at civilians began on February 26. By the end of the day, hundreds had been killed. That night soldiers of the Volynsky Guards Regiment,

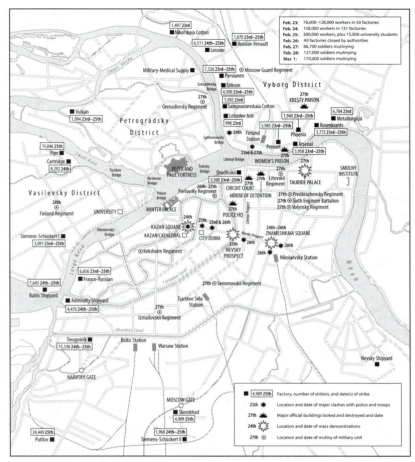

Map 3: Petrograd in February 1917

outraged at having been ordered to fire on unarmed civilians, resolved to mutiny. In the morning, they fanned out to other units and urged them to rebel. Many joined them and poured into the streets. Crowds destroyed symbols of Imperial authority. By midday, that authority was gone in Petrograd.

Victorious crowds proceeded to the only governmental body in the city whose authority they recognized—the Duma, which almost by default assumed power by forming a Provisional Committee. The revolutionary party leaders—especially Socialist-Revolutionaries and Mensheviks—simultaneously established the Petrograd Soviet of Worker

Deputies, soon joined by Petrograd soldiers, as a popular representative assembly. Its first official decree, Order Number One to the Petrograd garrison, de facto abolished the military chain of command (see Document 1.4).

Nicholas rushed back toward the capital, but rebellious railroad workers thwarted his return. On March 2, his leading generals convinced him to abdicate, in the hope of saving the war effort. Nicholas tried to pass the crown to his brother Mikhail, who rejected it. The Russian monarchy ended, and the Duma-appointed Provisional Government declared the dawn of a new era.

Initially the Provisional Government was composed of liberals and moderates—members of the Kadet and the Octobrist Parties—and one socialist (Alexander Kerensky; 1881–1970) and headed by Prince Georgii Lvov (1861–1925), a leading Zemstvo activist. One of the first acts of the Provisional Government was the abolition of the death penalty, considered a barbaric relic of the fallen regime. Most police institutions were also eliminated, political (and many regular) criminals freed, ethnic and religious discrimination banned, and full civil liberties proclaimed. The Provisional Government's main goal, however, was winning the war. Fundamental questions of state organization and popular issues like land reform were put off for an eventual Constituent Assembly to tackle.

The photograph shown in Figure 6 underscores that from the very outset, women activism was a crucial element in the February Revolution. Depicted is a women's demonstration in Petrograd on March 19. Marching along the city's main thoroughfare, Nevsky Prospekt, the demonstrators demanded electoral rights and political representation for women. The banners read: "A Women's Place is in the Constituent Assembly," "Strength is in Unity," and "Female Citizens of Free Russia Demand Electoral Rights." Under continued pressure, the Provisional Government granted women the right to vote on July 20. When the Russian Constituent Assembly finally met in Petrograd in January 1918, it became one of the first national representative bodies in the world elected on the basis of universal male and female suffrage.

The February Revolution was greeted as a welcome change by enthusiastic foreign observers (see Document 1.5). The British and French had grown apprehensive about espionage scandals and incessant rumors of German influence on Empress Alexandra and senior officials. The Russian military situation had been deteriorating, so it seemed that major

Figure 6: Women's demonstration in Petrograd on March
19, 1917. Source: TsGAKFFD Sankt-Peterburga.

political change could only be for the better. The United States' response
to the February Revolution was especially enthusiastic. For President
Wilson, the collapse of the autocratic regime facilitated his conception
of World War I as a war to promote democracy and "civilization." In his
message to Congress on April 4, Wilson proclaimed, "the great generous
Russian people have been added in all their naïve majesty and might to
the forces that are fighting for freedom in the world, for justice, and for
peace."[3]

Revolutionary reality in Russia, however, was far less tidy. Growing tensions emerged between the politically moderate Provisional Government,
which had claimed legislative and executive power, and the Petrograd
Soviet. Its socialist leaders pushed the government to seek a negotiated
settlement to the war and insisted that they represented the real source of
political legitimacy. The war's outcome and the success of the Revolution
itself, they believed, depended on the prompt democratization of society
and of the Imperial army, nor were they willing to accept deteriorating living conditions and the government's failure to improve them.

---

3. Quoted from Mario R. Dinunzio, ed., *Woodrow Wilson: Essential Writings and
Speeches of the Scholar-President* (New York and London: New York University Press,
2006), 401.

The Petrograd Soviet was far from the only popular organization claiming to champion the interests of the masses. A plethora of soviets and elected committees emerged in battalions and regiments, factories and towns, villages and provinces across the country, giving voice and power to millions of aggrieved people. Many localities and regions declared political autonomy. Industrial workers sought "worker control" over their factories. Peasant communes seized a huge number of private landholdings. Even many parishes declared their administrative autonomy from their dioceses. This unprecedented experiment in grassroots democracy was, however, accompanied by the collapse of infrastructure and established administrative bodies, economic disorganization, and waves of crime.

In the months following the February Revolution, the fragile consensus between the Provisional Government and the Petrograd Soviet, as well as other soviets, began to show signs of strain. The military victory that was supposed to bring the Great War to a close was nowhere to be seen, desertions from the Russian army increased, the transportation network grew more chaotic, inflation accelerated, and living standards continued to worsen. All of the blame fell on the Provisional Government.

Internationally, the Provisional Government struggled to find a middle ground between its great-power ambitions and the harsh reality of military defeats and nearly endless retreats. They tried to win Polish support with an offer of independence, a promise that could only be acted on after a German defeat (see Document 1.6). In the meantime, the Finns, Ukrainians, Georgians, Armenians, and other peoples continued to push for more autonomy or outright independence from Petrograd.

The German authorities facilitated the return from abroad of many revolutionary leaders, including Lenin, in the hope that they would undermine Russia's war effort. In fact, exiled and émigré activists of all stripes had been pouring into the capital. The day after his arrival, at the All-Russian Conference of Soviets of Workers' and Soldiers' Deputies, Lenin delivered his famous "April Theses" speech, calling for deepening the Revolution and the seizure of power by the soviets (see Document 1.7). At first the other Bolshevik leaders were skeptical, but as political and economic troubles multiplied, support for Lenin's program swelled.

The first major political crisis occurred on April 18, when Foreign Minister Miliukov's reassurance to the Allies of the Provisional Government's commitment to the war and expectation to receive control over the Dardanelles, and thus Constantinople, after its end became public. Massive anti-war rallies rocked Petrograd, forcing the government to shed

Figure 7: Kerensky in 1917

Miliukov and Guchkov, the Octobrist minister of war. Six socialists, who stood a better chance of working together with the soviets, now joined what was called "the First Coalition Government."

The Provisional Government's biggest effort to restore its standing among the increasingly disillusioned public was the June offensive against Austro-Hungarian and German forces in Galicia. Minister of War and Navy Alexander Kerensky (1881–1970) (see Figure 7), who had studied in the same gymnasium as Lenin and had once dreamed of killing the tsar, hoped the offensive would change the momentum of the war, reignite mass enthusiasm, take pressure off France, affirm Russia's place in the family of democratic nations, and silence the war's critics.

The offensive began on June 16 but collapsed two weeks later, resulting in tens of thousands of casualties. On July 3–7, mass protests, reminiscent of the February Days, erupted in Petrograd. The key slogan of the "July Days" was "All Power to the Soviets." Although Bolshevik activists had incited workers, sailors, and soldiers to protest, Lenin and his close associates refused to take the lead and the movement fizzled. The Provisional Government, supported by the Petrograd Soviet, dispersed the crowds by military force. Accused of being German agents, Lenin went into hiding and several Bolshevik leaders were jailed.

Yet the Provisional Government remained bitterly divided. On August 6 several Constitutional Democrats resigned. Kerensky headed up what now became "the Second Coalition Government." Even so, resentment towards the Provisional Government was turning into outright hatred at the frontlines and in the rear. Soldiers refused to follow orders and hundreds of thousands deserted. The Bolsheviks—who had steadfastly opposed the war and championed nationalizing gentry landholdings and worker control over factories—benefitted from the groundswell of public discontent. In Moscow, for example, they had won only 11.7 percent of the vote in city Duma elections in June, but 51 percent in elections to seventeen district Dumas in September.

In late August, Commander-in-Chief Lavr Kornilov (1870–1918) ordered his troops to move on Petrograd to restore order. He claimed he was acting on Kerensky's orders, while Kerensky charged him with mutiny. To defend Petrograd, Kerensky turned for assistance to the Petrograd Soviet, which in turn called out workers, soldiers, and sailors. Kornilov's assault was successfully halted, but this victory played into the hands of the Bolsheviks. By September, they were in control of the Petrograd Soviet with Leon Trotsky (1879–1940) at the helm (see Document 1.8). The Provisional Government went through another reshuffling and established a five-member "Directory," a reference to the government that took power in 1795 after the most radical phase of the French Revolution. Russia was formally declared a republic on September 1, and Kerensky now held supreme military and political power in the country. Or so it seemed. In reality, Russia was becoming increasingly ungovernable with fragmenting and shifting centers of power.

Lenin now was ready to call Kerensky's bluff, seize what was left of his power, and proceed with an ambitious socialist agenda. Intense debates took place among the Bolshevik leaders. Some argued that Russia was not ready to embrace socialism. Lenin countered that rural and weakly developed Russia could rely on the powerful industrial economies of Germany, France, and Britain to provide the needed push forward.

Russia's socialist revolution was a global event, he argued, the first salvo in the battle against world capitalism, soon to be followed by revolutions in Germany and elsewhere in Europe. The Bolsheviks' taking power in Russia, therefore, was in the interest of the international proletarian revolution.

Lenin's argument won the day. On October 24–25, the Bolsheviks used the Petrograd Soviet's Military-Revolutionary Committee, which had been created two weeks earlier for defense against the German advance on Petrograd and against counterrevolution, to seize control of power stations, communication centers, and other key sites in Petrograd. By the morning of October 25 (O.S.),[4] the Winter Palace—the seat of the Provisional Government—was the last remaining bastion. The cruiser Aurora fired a blank shell at the Winter Palace, followed by live shells shot by the guns of the Peter and Paul Fortress across the Neva River. Bolshevik supporters filtered into the Palace, gradually overpowering the defenders. Kerensky escaped to the front lines. The Bolshevik victory was complete. Even a casual look at the Bolshevik power-seizure, however, reveals major differences with the February Revolution (see Maps 3 and 4). Most important, hundreds of thousands of people flooded the streets in February, but only small bands came out in October. Yet similarities should not be overlooked. Both the Imperial Russian Government and the Provisional Government failed effectively to respond to pressing popular needs and could count on few committed defenders.

The Bolsheviks were soon joined by a left-wing splinter group of Socialist-Revolutionaries and formed a new government—the Council of People's Commissars (Sovnarkom), led by Lenin. He rejected even the term "ministers" to underscore the deep political rupture. Formally, the government was accountable to the All-Russian Congress of Soviets of Worker and Soldier Deputies, but the Bolsheviks quickly showed that they had little tolerance for political opposition, even in the soviets. They declared that their regime represented "a dictatorship of the proletariat," reserving to themselves the right to decide what the proletariat wanted.

The Bolsheviks' first decrees were decidedly populist. They immediately affirmed a desire to exit the war. This was a welcome relief to

---

4. As noted in the Preface, the Russian calendar until January 1918 followed the "Old Style" (O.S.), which in the twentieth century lagged thirteen days behind the Western, or Gregorian calendar, or "New Style" (N.S.).

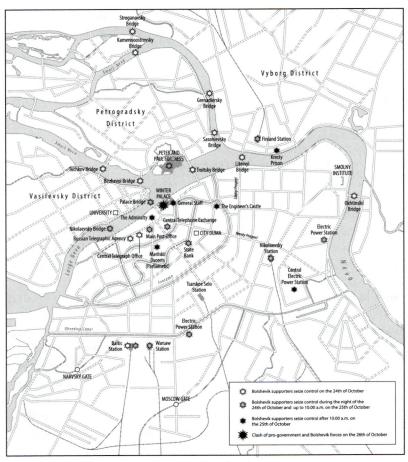

Map 4: Petrograd in October 1917

millions of Russian soldiers and sailors, peasants and workers who had suffered through meaningless slaughter. By that point, the multiethnic Russian Empire was already crumbling and scarcely capable of keeping up the fight. More than sixty self-styled independent territories appeared and disappeared in the post-Imperial space with exotic names like the Estland Workers' Commune, the Tanu-Tuvinsakaia Popular Republic, the Ural-Volga States of the Tatar and Bashkir Peoples, and the Rudobel'skaia Partisans' Republic.

Having embraced the Marxist ideology of class conflict and international working-class solidarity, the Bolsheviks simultaneously promoted the national liberation of all oppressed minorities, including those of the Russian Empire. On November 2, 1917, the Council of People's Commissars issued "the Declaration of the Rights of the Peoples' of Russia," which stressed their right to equality, self-determination, and even secession (see Document 1.9). This policy gave birth to a fusion of anti-capitalist and anti-colonial rhetoric, which broadened the Bolsheviks' appeal and, in the soon-to-follow Civil War, severely undermined the position of their adversaries, whose support for the restoration of a unified Russian state found little enthusiasm in the Empire's ethnically diverse periphery. But in their own state-building efforts, the Bolsheviks sacrificed national self-determination for the imperatives of political control. This quickly became clear, for example, from the situation in Turkestan—a vast central Asian region that had come under Imperial Russian control in the late nineteenth century (see Document 1.10).

The Bolsheviks also nationalized all the land and sanctioned its use by peasants, de facto approving peasant seizures of estates that had been occurring since the summer. Most important, their coming to power meant to the Bolsheviks that the global transition from capitalism to communism had begun. What exactly the new world would look like, no one was sure. Karl Marx's writings on communism were scanty (especially when compared to *Das Kapital*, his three-volume study of capitalism). Theoretically, communism was supposed to unleash the creative potential of mankind, allowing it to attain ever-growing levels of economic productivity, inventiveness, and freedom. It was not just a socioeconomic concept of modernization, but also an inspirational vision that captivated the minds of Marx's followers (see Document 1.11).

But how could it be achieved? The Bolsheviks set out by and large on their own. They immediately abolished social ranks, titles, and privileges. From governmental policies pursued by the major powers during the Great War, they adopted centralized control over the economy and society. From socialist theory, they took for granted the need to eliminate private property and the market and to take charge of the economy. They expected to unleash the workers' support and enthusiasm, yet did not shrink from imposing on them the strictest organization, discipline, and control (see Document 1.12). Certain that they alone understood the inner workings of social development, they devoted huge resources to education and propaganda—but also relied on censorship, coercion, and violence, especially when it turned out that most of Russian society did not share their revolutionary agenda.

As the soviets were gradually purged of non-Bolshevik socialists—Mensheviks, Socialist-Revolutionaries, and even Left Socialist-Revolutionaries—the term "Soviet power" became synonymous with the Bolshevik regime and one-party rule. The freely elected Constituent Assembly, in which the Bolsheviks received only a quarter of the seats, was dissolved at gunpoint on the night of January 5–6, 1918, after only one day in session.

Within a few months, the Bolsheviks alienated growing numbers of people who objected to their radical vision and policies—from government officials and Imperial army officers, to educated elites and moderate socialist party activists, to peasants branded "kulaks" for protesting forced grain requisitions and even workers who lost the right to strike. In fact, the Bolshevik failure to share power and adjust their radical policies made a devastating civil war virtually unavoidable.

By summer 1918, the Bolsheviks, or the "Reds," were surrounded on almost all sides, but benefitted from control of Russia's heartland, main railroad lines, and main industrial centers, as well as from their ruthlessly centralized and state-driven approach to the economy (see Map 5). Their opponents, generally referred to as the "Whites," often had little in common with one another except for hatred of the Reds. The main White forces were dominated by former Imperial officers and led by General Anton Denikin in the South and Admiral Aleksandr Kolchak in the East. The Whites' political views ranged from monarchist to socialist, and they had to contend with national minorities demanding regional autonomy, disgruntled landlords hoping to get their land back, liberal politicians calling for the restoration of civil liberties, and socialist political activists quarreling over peasant and labor policies (see Document 1.13).

The Bolsheviks' effort to build the Red Army was spearheaded by Leon Trotsky, who proved to be a remarkably successful military organizer despite a lack of professional training. Discipline was fierce: military professionals were forcibly recruited, millions of peasants were conscripted, and deserters were hunted down. The Bolsheviks did not hesitate to use violence and terror throughout the Civil War era. In the early morning of July 17, 1918, as discussed above, Bolshevik operatives in Ekaterinburg in the Ural Mountains slaughtered the entire Imperial family—Nicholas, Alexandra, their five children, and their servants—in cold blood and without warning. The next day, several more Imperial family members were also murdered.

Faced with Bolshevik disregard for democracy and increasingly ruthless treatment of the peasantry, the Socialist-Revolutionaries agonized over how to confront their revolutionary brothers-in-arms. Should they work within the new political system? Or should they fight the Bolsheviks as new tyrants, using violence and terror? On August 30, proponents of the latter tactic killed the head of the Petrograd Security Police (Cheka) Moisei Uritskii (1873–1918) and badly wounded Lenin in Moscow. In response, the Bolsheviks proclaimed the "Red Terror." Rejecting the principle of individual culpability, they declared all representatives of the "bourgeois exploitative classes" responsible. Tens of thousands of merchants, priests, officers, intellectuals, and wealthy peasants were held hostage, sent to concentration camps, or killed. The Bolsheviks continued to use this tactic in the course of the Civil War. They played on the popular hatred for the vaguely defined "bourgeoisie," but also genuinely believed that the Red Terror would not only intimidate and deter their enemies, but also speed up the dawn of a classless society.

The sailors who had mostly supported the Bolsheviks in 1917 and the industrial workers whose interests they supposedly represented also suffered repression. In 1921, when sailors and workers at the naval fortress of Kronstadt in the Gulf of Finland demanded "socialism without the Bolsheviks," democratic elections to the Soviets, and various civil liberties, the government crushed the "uprising" with massive firepower and brutal repression, resulting in thousands of deaths (see Document 3.6).

Modern propaganda played a key role in the Bolsheviks' mass mobilization efforts. Using print, images, audio recordings, radio broadcasts, and even movies, they called upon their supporters to help "save the proletarian revolution" against the dark forces of "bourgeoisie." Workers and peasants could easily relate such rhetoric to personal experiences of exploitation and oppression, even more so since in the course of the Civil War the Whites perpetrated a large share of atrocities, including massive anti-Jewish pogroms.

The White leaders attempted to promote their own propaganda, but with less success, due in part to the sheer diversity of their views and interests. The posters shown in Figures 8 and 9 both use the ubiquitous

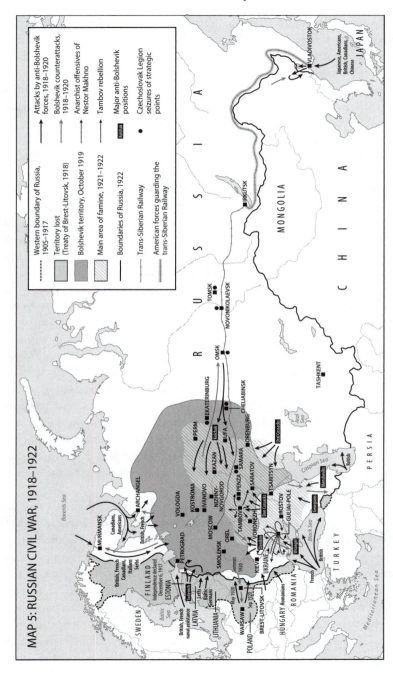

MAP 5: RUSSIAN CIVIL WAR, 1918–1922

"I Want You" appeal, first conceived by the British at the beginning of World War I.[5] While the White poster was a toned-down version of a 1917 Italian poster by Luciano Mauzan, the Bolshevik poster by Dmitrii Moor displayed original artistry, made reference to ordinary people and the importance of factory workers, and therefore was generally more compelling in the context of the Civil War. Ultimately, the Bolsheviks prevailed not only because of their ruthlessness and discipline, but also because of their captivating vision of the future that inspired ordinary people to commit acts of selfless sacrifice and heroism (see Document 1.14).

Even so, the conscious efforts of both the Reds and the Whites to cast the Civil War in bipolar terms masked the diversity of colliding attitudes and interests. Most importantly, the peasantry, the vast majority of the population, never fully embraced either side: hostile to Bolshevik food requisition policies but also fearful lest the landlords return and reclaim their lands, peasants deserted by the millions from the mass-conscripted armies of both sides and sometimes mutinied—occasionally referring to themselves as "the Greens"—against any external authority that sought to control their resources. The Bolsheviks in particular faced a series of peasant uprisings in Ukraine, the Volga region, south-central Russia, and Siberia, which erupted most powerfully after the Whites had been defeated in 1920. The Bolsheviks brutally crushed these uprisings (see Document 1.15). Forced requisitioning of grain and poor weather caused a tragic famine in 1921–1922, resulting in at least 1.5 to 2 million deaths. Nor did the cities escape the ravages of Civil War and the extreme economic centralization of War Communism. For example, the population of Petrograd plummeted from 2.5 million in 1917 to 722,000 in 1920, while the number of industrial workers more than halved from 2.6 to 1.2 million. As a result, industrial output collapsed, falling 69 percent from 1913 to 1921.[6]

The Bolsheviks never viewed the Civil War as a purely domestic problem. Instead they saw it in the context of a class struggle that knew no borders. A peasant who took up arms to defend his livestock and a US

---

5. See Alfred Leete, "Your Country Needs YOU," *London Opinion*, September 5, 1914, p. 1.

6. See Lewis H. Siegelbaum, *Soviet State and Society Between Revolutions, 1918–1929* (Cambridge and New York: Cambridge University Press, 1992), 27; Alec Nove, *An Economic History of the USSR*, 2d ed. (London: Penguin Books, 1989), 57–58.

| Figure 8: "Have You Enlisted as a Volunteer?" (1920) | Figure 9: "Why Are You Not in the Army?" (1919) |

president who reluctantly authorized military intervention in Russia were one and the same enemy—"the bourgeois class," whose universal destruction, they believed, was the only way to ensure the global triumph of communism and the advent of a world of genuine human happiness, free from exploitation, inequality, and injustice. This was going to be a struggle for the future of mankind. The following section will focus on Soviet Russia's interaction with the world and on the Bolsheviks' evolving foreign policy approaches and objectives in relation to that paramount vision and goal.

The Bolsheviks Engage the World

The Bolsheviks were not the first political actors in Russia who played up the international ramifications of the Revolution. From the first days of its existence, the Provisional Government leaders hoped that revolutionary change in Russia would help bring the Great War to a victorious end for the Allied Powers, which now fully looked like a family of democratic nations. On March 27, the Petrograd Soviet took this thinking even further by issuing an appeal "to the peoples of the whole world." The appeal declared that the "Russian democracy has shattered in the dust the age-long despotism of the Tsar and enters your family [of nations] as an equal, and as a mighty force in the struggle for our common liberation." It then called on all peoples, and first and foremost the German proletariat, "to begin a decisive struggle with the acquisitive aspirations of the governments of other countries."[7] The appeal admonished German workers specifically to follow the example of the Russian Revolution and overthrow "the yoke of your semi-autocratic rule…refuse to serve as an instrument of conquest and violence in the hands of kings, landowners, and bankers." The Russian Revolution made a global impact even before the Bolsheviks seized power. But it was the Bolsheviks, the final victors of the Russian Revolution, who advanced their vision of it on an unprecedented scale.

To practically minded Bolsheviks like Lenin, the international significance of the Russian Revolution depended on whether it could trigger other communist revolutions in Europe and provide real-world lessons for how to make them successful. Initially, the Bolsheviks were highly optimistic on both counts, and their foreign policy grew out of that optimism. They developed a unique approach to foreign relations because their revolutionary goals were unique and unprecedented in history. But what specifically did they seek to achieve, where, and when? What methods and tools did they use? What intended and unintended consequences resulted from their foreign policy and how much did it actually help revolutionize the world?

At the time when the Bolsheviks seized power, states had been recognized for nearly 300 years, since the end of the Thirty Years' War (1618–1648), as the main actors in foreign relations. Concomitantly, serving state interests (also conceptualized as "national interests" in nation-states) was seen as an overarching principle of diplomacy. The Bolsheviks had deliberately smashed the Imperial Russian state and at first were not sure what, if anything, should replace it. The broad declaratory nature of their first decrees, their willingness to proceed with the elections to the Constituent Assembly, and their destruction of key legal, political, social, and economic institutions indicate their initial hopefulness and optimism about the spontaneous revolutionary energy of the masses. They soon realized, however, that this energy alone did not suffice to bring about

---

7. Excerpted from Alfred Golder, ed., *Documents of Russian History, 1914–1917*, trans. Emanuel Aronsberg (New York: The Century Co., 1927), 325–26.

the broad changes they believed necessary to move Russia towards socialism. By 1918, the Bolsheviks were striving to ensure party dominance
throughout the country in local soviets, never hesitating to dissolve them
and arrest their opponents or even replace them altogether with military-revolutionary committees directly subordinated to Moscow, which
became Soviet Russia's capital in the spring of 1918. Within the party,
the Bolsheviks stressed centralization and discipline, with key decision-
making power in the hands of the Central Committee and increasingly
concentrated in the Politburo, its small executive board. They also set up
and continuously expanded the power of the All-Russian Extraordinary
Commission (the Cheka), the security police, to fight counterrevolution,
sabotage, speculation, and other "counterrevolutionary" crimes. They
took steps to build a new army and a new administrative apparatus. In
sum, they came to believe that the transition to socialism could only be
achieved by means of a new "proletarian" state and state institutions.

Yet the concept of "state interest" does not adequately explain Bolshevik foreign policy and its methods and goals. The Bolsheviks' view of the
Soviet state was ambiguous at best. The state to them was an important,
but transitory construction. They expected revolution to engulf other
European countries at any moment and thus to liberate the working
classes there. Once triumphant, the working classes of the world would
not even need the machinery of the state, which was expected "to wither
away," as humanity moved towards communism. The party's new name,
picked in spring 1918 ("the Russian Communist Party [Bolsheviks]"),
underscored their commitment to the worldwide communist movement.
Grigorii Zinoviev (1883–1936), a leading Bolshevik and the party leader
of the Petrograd region, conveyed well this almost millenarian anticipation in a statement he made in 1919:

> Old Europe is dashing at a mad speed towards the proletarian
> revolution.
>
> …Occasional defeats will still occur in the near future. The
> color black will perhaps win a victory here and there over
> the color red. But the final victory will, nevertheless, go to
> the color red; and this in the span of months, perhaps even
> weeks. The movement is proceeding at such terrific speed
> that we may say with full confidence that within a year we
> shall already begin to forget that there was a struggle for com-
> munism in Europe, because in a year the whole of Europe will

have become communist. And the struggle for communism
will be transferred to America, perhaps to Asia, and to other
parts of the world.

　　. . .

It may happen that in America capitalism will continue for a
few years to subsist side by side with Communist Europe. It
may happen that even in England capitalism may continue
to exist for a year or two, side by side with communism
victorious in the whole of continental Europe. But such a
co-existence cannot last long. . . .[8]

In other words, even though the Bolsheviks created a new state, they did
not develop a strong allegiance to it. Their primary allegiance was to revolution, as they defined it.

　　Domestically, this revolution gave birth to their regime, which they
called and was popularly known as "Soviet power." Internationally, the
revolution was going to launch a new phase in human history. Implied
in Bolshevik thinking about revolution was not a state or a nation whose
interests had to be pursued, but "an imagined community" of a very different kind—a global community of the masses with a shared experience
of exploitation. Revolution meant the liberation of this community led
by industrial workers, led in turn by revolutionary Marxists. The Bolsheviks' allegiance to this community superseded their allegiance to the
Soviet state. In diplomatic terms, this meant that, from the outset, Bolshevik foreign policy was driven primarily not by state interest, but by
what can be defined as "revolutionary interest."

　　The conflict and tension over the roles and meanings of revolutionary
and state interests were more profound than the rivalry between different branches of the Bolshevik foreign policy apparatus, nor was it iden-
tical to the frequently discussed ideological versus pragmatic divide in
Soviet foreign policy.[9] Various policies driven by revolutionary or state

---

8. G. Zinoviev, "Die Perspectiven der proletarischen Revolution," *Die Kommunistische
Internationale*, no. 1 (August 1919), ix–xiv [here: xii, xiv].

9. See, for example, Gabriel Gorodetsky, "The Formulation of Soviet Foreign Policy—
Ideology and *Realpolitik*" in Gabriel Gorodetsky, ed., *Soviet Foreign Policy, 1917–1991:
A Retrospective* (London and Portland, OR: Frank Cass, 1994), 30–44; Michael Jabara
Carley, *Silent Conflict: A Hidden History of Early Soviet-Western Relations* (Lanham,
MD: Rowman & Littlefield, 2014), Preface.

interest could involve a certain dose of ideology, as well as pragmatism. But they were rooted in different expectations of the world's future: eager anticipation of an imminent global revolutionary triumph resulted in the dominance of the revolutionary interest; the decline of revolutionary movements abroad led to the assertion of the state interest.

The first period of Soviet foreign policy, marked by the primacy of revolutionary interest, grew out of Lenin's initial expectations of a global socialist revolution in the fall of 1917. On October 1, as he sought to convince other party leaders to seize power, he pointed to the execution of German sailors (most likely for their participation in a recent mutiny in Wilhelmshaven, a coastal German city on the North Sea)."The beginning of the revolution is obvious," he wrote, stressing the urgent need to secure the world revolution, the Russian Revolution, and "the lives of hundreds of thousands of people at the front."[10]

The same sentiment was reflected in the first Bolshevik decree—the Decree on Peace. Adopted on October 26, it called for an immediate armistice between all warring powers and for the relinquishing of claims on all "annexed" territories overseas as well as in Europe. The decree, it was hoped, would appeal not just to governments, but to peoples around the world, and in particular to the "conscious workers" of what the leading Bolsheviks considered the three most advanced nations: England, France, and Germany. These workers, according to the decree, had the task "to secure the cause of peace along with the cause of liberating the working and exploited masses of population from all slavery and all exploitation."[11] According to the Bolsheviks, genuine peace was impossible without the defeat of capitalist imperialism and the revolutionary transformation of the world. The Decree on Peace was therefore also a decree on world revolution.

The primacy of the revolutionary interest at this point was nearly total, so that the Bolsheviks, eager to reach out to the exploited masses over the heads of the governments, did not see a need to resort to traditional tools of state diplomacy. When Leon Trotsky, having played a critical role at the helm of the Petrograd Soviet, was appointed Commissar of Foreign Affairs, he thought of it as a small job: "I will issue

---

10. Vladimir Lenin, "Letter to the Central Committee, the Moscow and Petrograd Committees and the Bolshevik Members of the Petrograd and Moscow Soviets," *Collected Works*, vol. 26 (Moscow: Progress Publishers, 1964), 140–41.

11. *Dekrety sovetskoi vlasti*, 18 vols. (Moscow: Gospolitizdat, 1957), 1:12.

Figure 10: "Death to World Imperialism!" (1919)

Figure 11: "Comrade Lenin Clears the Earth of Filth" (1920)

a few revolutionary proclamations to the peoples of the world and then shut up shop."[12]

Trotsky began by publishing secret correspondence and agreements between the Allied powers regarding postwar territorial changes in Europe and the partition of the Ottoman Empire. He declared abolition of secret diplomacy and its "intrigues, codes, and lies."[13] But his job soon grew bigger. When Russia's allies refused to respond to the Decree on Peace, the Bolsheviks turned to the Central Powers. A unilateral armistice on the Eastern Front was signed on November 24, 1917, and on December 9 peace talks between Russia and the Central Powers began in the city of Brest-Litovsk (see Document 2.1). These negotiations soon broke down. Germany, because of its position of great military strength compared to Russia, whose army had practically collapsed, demanded from the Bolsheviks big territorial concessions. Trotsky, as the head of

---

12. As quoted in E. H. Carr, *The Bolshevik Revolution, 1917–1923*, 3 vols. (New York and London: W. W. Norton & Company, 1985), 3:16.

13. Lev Trotsky, *Sochineniia* (Moscow-Leningrad: Gosizdat, 1925), vol. 3, pt. 2, p. 167.

the Soviet delegation, refused. He was motivated not by imperial ambition, but by the leading Bolsheviks' belief that a German revolution would soon sweep away the kaiser's regime. The armistice was thus broken. The German offensive, re-launched on February 18, 1918, proved to be unstoppable by military means. The Bolsheviks had to return to the negotiating table. Thus it was only with great reluctance and only when faced with a profound existential threat that the Bolsheviks accommodated state interests in their early foreign policy. Even their most ardent proponents viewed these accommodations as tactical retreats.

The terms of the Treaty of Brest-Litovsk, signed on March 3, 1918, were severe. As illustrated in Map 5 (p. 26), Soviet Russia ceded control over vast territories that had been part of the Russian Empire, shedding a quarter of its population and industry. Although the Treaty of Brest-Litovsk was abrogated when a defeated Germany was forced to sign the Treaty of Versailles the following year, its political and psychological impact on Russia was lasting and continues to this day.

Immediately after Soviet Russia formally exited the Great War, British troops landed in the far-northern Russian seaport of Murmansk. The British hoped to protect accumulated military supplies, to fend off a German-Finnish attempt to capture the Murmansk-Petrograd railroad, and also to continue the fight alongside the Bolsheviks against the Central Powers. In addition, they hoped that the 50,000-strong Czechoslovak Legion, which had been fighting with the Russian Army against the Austrians, would depart from Russia and join the Allied forces. At first the Bolsheviks were willing to collaborate, but on May 13, Lenin succeeded in convincing his fellow party leaders to comply with German demands to disarm the Czechoslovak forces. As a result, the Czechoslovak troops, which had been traveling eastward on the Trans-Siberian Railway in order to circle the globe and join the fight on the Western Front, rebelled and quickly seized control of several cities from the Volga River to western Siberia.

Western historians have often downplayed the significance of Allied intervention forces in Russia, pointing to their limited objectives and small scale. Indeed, the number of British troops in the Far North never exceeded eight thousand, but the Czechoslovak revolt showed what even relatively small numbers of well-organized, trained, and disciplined troops could accomplish. The cascading impact of the Czechoslovak revolt was catastrophic for the Bolsheviks. In summer 1918, almost the whole of Siberia, the Ural Mountains, and the Volga region slipped from their control. Many Allied leaders hoped this development would lead to the toppling of the Bolshevik government by their Civil War adversaries, which might reopen the eastern front against the Central Powers.[14]

Over the summer, the scope of foreign intervention widened. The largest expeditionary force was sent by Japan, eventually reaching 70,000 men in Siberia. The American Expeditionary Forces landed in the northern seaport of Archangelsk (5,000 troops) as well as in the Pacific port of Vladivostok (roughly 8,000 troops). General William Sidney Graves (1865–1940) commanded the latter from September 1918 until their evacuation in 1920. The mandate of the American Expeditionary Force in Siberia was extremely limited: to protect allied military supplies and ensure safe passage and evacuation of Czechoslovak troops from Russia via the Trans-Siberian Railroad. Graves's orders precluded him from rendering active support to any party in the Civil War. Graves himself was a reluctant interventionist and believed that "there isn't a nation on earth that would not resent foreigners sending troops into their country, for the purpose of putting this or that faction in charge of their Government machinery."[15] While in Siberia, Graves grew further convinced of this, having witnessed numerous abuses committed by Cossack warlords who were loosely associated with Admiral Aleksandr Kolchak (1874–1920), the supreme commander of the anti-Bolshevik Siberian government (see Document 2.4).

Graves's caution notwithstanding, growing Allied involvement in Russian affairs reinforced the Bolsheviks' class-based worldview, which saw the international bourgeoisie coalescing in its vicious desire to crush the first proletarian state. For the second time in six months the Bolsheviks were confronted with an existential threat.

At this point, the Bolshevik foray into state-interest diplomacy (seeking to establish formal relations and using the language of diplomatic notes) resulted from the dire necessity to use any tools at their disposal to ensure the survival of the Russian Revolution, as they saw it (see Document 2.2). In their broader worldview, the Russian Revolution could be secured only through a complete recasting of the world's social, economic, and political structures. This in turn was predicated on a global revolutionary triumph

---

14. See Ian C. D. Moffat, *The Allied Intervention in Russia, 1918–1920: The Diplomacy of Chaos* (Houndmills, Basingstoke, Hampshire: Palgrave Macmillan, 2015).

15. William S. Graves, *America's Siberian Adventure, 1918–1920* (New York: Cape Ann Smith, 1931), 82.

and the elimination of the very international actors, or states, with which the Bolsheviks engaged in diplomacy. This made international conflict more important than peace and stability in their thinking about international relations. The tactical imperative to engage "the old world" clashed with the strategic imperative to destroy it and led to a constant search for ingenious foreign policy solutions. The result was an approach to international relations as unique and revolutionary as Soviet Russia itself.

Fundamentally, it was an optimistic approach. The Bolsheviks believed that time was on their side in their confrontation with "the old world," if they could only hold on to power during a fairly short interval. This short-term goal required not only domestic military and economic mobilization, but international mobilization as well—reaching out to the working classes all over the world, inspiring their sympathy and support for Soviet Russia. For this purpose, the Bolshevik leadership relied on propaganda as much as on diplomacy. At the very least, they hoped such an approach would make it much harder for foreign governments to intervene in Soviet Russia's affairs (see Document 2.3).

Then, on October 1, 1918, when the collapse of the German monarchy seemed imminent amid chaos and growing revolutionary turmoil, Lenin advocated providing German workers with all possible grain and military assistance and conscripting a three-million-man army to assist the international worker revolution. In his words: "We are all ready to die to help the German workers deepen the revolution they have begun."[16] The greater was his disappointment when most German Social Democrats opted for the creation of a parliamentary republic instead of immediately moving toward a Bolshevik-style system.

Still, to the Bolsheviks, revolution in Europe seemed just around the corner. In Germany they encouraged the radical socialist Spartacist League led by Karl Liebknecht (1871–1919) and Rosa Luxemburg (1871–1919). In January 1919, the League tried to seize power in Berlin, but failed. Bolshevik hopes spiked again when, in March, Hungarian socialists and communists proclaimed the creation of a Hungarian Soviet Republic. By this point the Bolsheviks were thinking more boldly about how to promote world revolution. They knew that their own victory in Russia required strategic direction, discipline, and organization, so they tried to impart these principles to communist leaders on an international scale (see Document 2.5).

---

16. V. I. Lenin to Ia. M. Sverdlov and L. D. Trotskii, in *PSS*, 50:185–86 [here: 186].

The Communist International (Comintern), founded in Moscow in early March 1919, was to become to the world revolution what the Bolshevik party was to the Russian Revolution.[17] Also called "the Third International" to distinguish it from the moderate Second Socialist International (1889–1916), which collapsed during the Great War, the Comintern brought together communist parties from all over the world. The Comintern's mission was to assist and coordinate their efforts to spread the world revolution. This mission was proclaimed even as the Bolsheviks were in the midst of the Civil War, fighting for survival against the forces of Anton Denikin in the south and Aleksandr Kolchak in the east.

Bolshevik victory in this struggle was followed by another war, this time launched by Poland. The Polish-Soviet War of spring and summer 1920 revealed the Bolsheviks' continuing commitment to the revolutionary interest. In the early phases of the war, Polish forces successfully occupied Kiev as the Bolsheviks scrambled to rebuff them. Within months, however, the military fortunes changed, and the Red Army went on the offensive. Now, the Bolsheviks' dream of the world revolution was re-ignited. The offensive was conducted in large part, according to Lenin, "to probe with a bayonet the readiness of Poland for social revolution."[18] War to the Bolshevik leaders was one of many tools, which could be used at the right moment and in the right place, to help liberate the world's oppressed masses from the shackles of capitalist exploitation.

When Red Army troops were nearing Warsaw in July 1920, the Second Congress of the Comintern opened in Moscow. The Congress took a major step towards implementing the Bolshevik model of revolutionary activism on a global scale by passing twenty-one conditions for membership, including the obligation to adhere to organizational discipline and to give unconditional support to every soviet republic throughout the world in its struggle against the forces of counterrevolution.

Even though the Bolsheviks established diplomatic relations with the Baltic states and pursued trade relations with England, this conventional state-interest diplomacy remained subordinate to the overarching

---

17. See Duncan Hallas, *The Comintern* (Chicago: Haymarket Books, 2008).

18. Richard Pipes, ed., *The Unknown Lenin: From the Secret Archive*, with the assistance of David Brandenberger (New Haven and London: Yale University Press, 1996), 100.

revolutionary agenda. Increasingly, then, Bolshevik opponents in Europe and in America viewed Soviet Russia as a sinister and insidious power bent on global subversion and conquest. Bolshevism was seen as a disease and in the words of the French Prime Minister Georges Clemenceau (1841–1929), required a "cordon sanitaire," or "sanitary barrier," made of the newly independent countries of eastern Europe to prevent its spread. The British government was more optimistic. On February 10, 1920, Premier David Lloyd George, in a speech before the House of Commons, asserted: "Commerce has a sobering influence. There is nothing to fear from a Bolshevist invasion of surrounding countries...because the Bolsheviki cannot organize a powerful army. I believe that trading will bring to an end the ferocity, rapine, and cruelty of Bolshevism more surely than any other method."[19]

By September 1920, the Poles had rolled the Red Army back from Polish territory and had forced the Bolsheviks to accept an expanded Poland. Still, the Bolshevik domestic and foreign positions were strong and stable. In November, their military forces crushed the last bulwark of White resistance in the Crimea. Abroad, the Comintern was developing into an effective tool to coordinate revolutionary efforts (see Document 2.6).

Soviet stabilization, however, coincided with general European stabilization and the decline of revolutionary activity. This forced the Bolsheviks to reevaluate their revolutionary tactics and the temporal horizon for the world revolution (see Document 2.7). By extension, they also had to reconsider their perspective on the Soviet state. It appeared that the state, not world revolution, was here to stay, and, at least in the near future, would have to function on its own in a hostile capitalist environment. In these conditions, survival, security, and economic development dictated a greater emphasis on state interest in foreign relations.

Late 1920 through early 1921 marked the beginning of a new phase in Soviet foreign policy based on an unsteady equilibrium between revolutionary and state interests. Speaking to the Eighth Congress of Soviets in December 1920, Lenin admitted that while it would be "most pleasant to defeat all the imperialist powers," the strength of the capitalist world and Soviet Russia's geopolitical isolation required playing on disagreements between imperialist powers.[20] In March 1921,

---

19. "Lloyd George's Program," *The Independent* (New York; February 21, 1920), 286.

20. *PSS*, 5:105.

the government announced the moderate pro-market New Economic Policy at home and the Anglo-Soviet Trade Agreement abroad—the first major Soviet diplomatic breakthrough with a leading western state, in this case England. Retreating from the primacy of revolutionary interest facilitated a series of agreements, signed by the Bolsheviks, allowing the Red Cross, the American Relief Administration, and other international humanitarian organizations to bring desperately needed food and medical supplies to the famine-stricken areas of the Volga and Ural regions in 1921–22. Food aid from abroad saved millions of lives; despite this help, at least 1.5 to 2 million people died of starvation and famine-related disease.

The first wide-ranging exercise of state-interest diplomacy took place when, in 1922, the Soviets agreed to attend the Genoa Conference convened in Italy to discuss issues of European economic recovery, Soviet debt obligations, and trade.[21] Representatives of Soviet Russia and Weimar Germany met separately in Rappalo, where they signed an agreement that cancelled out reciprocal claims for war damages and territory, established diplomatic relations between the two countries, and promoted economic, political, and (thanks to a subsequent secret pact signed on July 29, 1922) extensive military cooperation (see Document 2.8).[22] In May 1922, the Bolshevik Central Committee adopted a resolution, declaring "the whole course of international relations recently bears witness to the inevitability, at the present stage of historical development, of the temporary co-existence of the communist and bourgeois systems of property."[23]

In the same year, when state interests began to reassert themselves, the Soviet state itself underwent a major change with the creation of the Union of Soviet Socialist Republics, a polity revolutionary in structure,

---

21. Over 800 journalists attended the conference including Ernest Hemingway for the *Toronto Star*, Wickham Steed for the *Times*, and M. Keynes for the *Manchester Guardian*. The conference was called the "largest gathering of European statesmen since the Crusades." See Stephen White, *The Origins of Detente. The Genoa Conference and Soviet-Western Relations 1921–1922* (Cambridge: Cambridge University Press, 1985), 255.

22. On subsequent Soviet-German cooperation, see Aleksandr Nekrich, *Pariahs, Partners, Predators: German-Soviet Relations, 1922–1941* (New York: Columbia University Press, 1997).

23. Quoted in Jon Jacobson, *When the Soviet Union Entered World Politics* (Berkeley: University of California Press, 1994), 26.

as well as in aspiration. By 1922, the Bolsheviks were in control of Ukraine, Belorussia, Georgia, Armenia, and Azerbaijan. The latter three republics were merged during the course of 1922 into the Transcaucasian Socialist Federative Soviet Republic, which the Bolshevik central party leaders had initially planned to unite, along with Ukraine and Belorussia, into Soviet Russia, with autonomy only in matters of local governance. Lenin, however, was becoming increasingly alarmed about a possible resurgence of Russian nationalism and a de facto inferior status for national minorities within the larger Soviet state. His ambitious solution was to create an entirely new union of formally equal socialist republics. The centralized economy and political authority of the Bolshevik leadership in Moscow was to be maintained, yet administratively member republics would retain delineated borders and partially autonomous political and administrative institutions. In practice, the level of actual autonomy was very modest. The creation of the new Union of Soviet Socialist Republics, at the end of December 1922, thus finalized the revolutionary destruction of the Russian Empire with its provincial administrative organization. It also left the door open to the incorporation of new members, for the Bolsheviks expected the revolution to spread further. On December 30, 1922, the First Congress of Soviets of the Union of Soviet Socialist Republics approved a Declaration on the formation of the USSR. The Declaration stressed that the USSR would serve as "a reliable bulwark against world capitalism" but at the same time would be "a new decisive step on the path of unifying the working people of all countries into the Global Socialist Soviet Republic."[24]

The Great Seal of the USSR, adopted in 1923, represented the new state. It boasted a globe, a rising sun, the motto: "Proletarians of All Countries Unite!" from the *Communist Manifesto* (1848), and a hammer and sickle to represent the unity of the workers and the peasants. Ironically, the first version (Figure 12) contained a glaring error that was corrected only in the 1937 revision (Figure 13): the handle of the sickle was depicted upside down, a feature any peasant would have noticed instantly. The banners proclaimed the Soviet motto in the various languages of the

---

24. A. S. Orlov, ed., *Khrestomatiia po istorii Rossii s drevneishikh vremen do nashikh dnei* (Moscow: Prospekt, 1999), 224.

Figure 12: Great Seal of the USSR (1923)

Figure 13: Great Seal of the USSR (1937)

constituent republics of the USSR, which had increased from six to eleven during the intervening years.

Ensuring the security of the fledgling Soviet state and rebuilding the war-ravaged and deindustrialized economy were major concerns for the Bolsheviks in the 1920s. During these years, the Soviet leaders incessantly pursued diplomatic recognition and commercial opportunities from "the capitalist world." These efforts yielded both setbacks and successes. Britain officially recognized the Soviet Union in 1924, France did so in 1925, and the United States, belatedly, followed suit in 1933. This shift in Bolshevik priorities empowered the diplomacy-driven People's Commissariat of Foreign Affairs, whose head, Georgii Chicherin (1872–1936), worried about diplomatic risks of Comintern's revolutionary approach to foreign relations. Trade also increased, but on Bolshevik terms. A state monopoly on foreign trade was established in April 1918, followed by the creation of several state agencies for trade with Western countries, including the All-Russian Co-operative Society (ARCOS) in London in 1920 and the American Trade Corporation (AMTORG) in New York in 1924. These wholly state-controlled front organizations became important actors in the Soviet foreign relations apparatus. Generally, foreign trade was meant to focus on rebuilding and modernizing Soviet Russia's industrial base, not importing consumer products. Exports peaked in 1930 at 3.612 million rubles and imports in 1931 at

3.851 million rubles in constant 1950 rubles,[25] before declining in the course of the Great Depression.

While state interests were gaining ground, revolutionary interests remained a prominent factor in Soviet foreign policy in the course of the 1920s. The People's Commissariat of Foreign Affairs was treated as a technical advisory board by the Politburo leaders, who were unwilling to give up their commitment to worldwide revolutionary transformation by means of the Comintern in exchange for the normalization of diplomatic relations. Chicherin compared such a concession to a pope giving up the Catholic Church.[26]

These competing interests clashed in 1923 when, in response to Germany's failure to pay war reparations, France occupied the industrial Ruhr Valley. The initial Soviet response was driven by state interests. French domination of Germany could pose a potential threat to the USSR, so the Soviets condemned the French action, warned Poland not to get involved, and expressed general support for the Weimar government. Then the German Communist Party called for general strike, which was followed by revolutionary turmoil in Thuringia, Saxony, and Hamburg. Once more it seemed that Europe, or at least Germany, was moving towards revolution. The Bolsheviks were faced with a dilemma: Should they promote revolution in Germany, which would undermine the Weimar government, or focus on diplomacy, because a strong Weimar Republic benefited Soviet state security? They opted for the former. Speaking to party activists in Moscow on September 29, Zinoviev boldly asserted, "events in Germany are opening a new page in the history of world revolution."[27] Days earlier, the Politburo and the Central Committee, having explored the tantalizing prospects of a Soviet Germany's alliance with the USSR and the eventual creation of "a Union of Soviet Republics of Europe and Asia," proclaimed that "the interests of the USSR in the

---

25. See Appendix B in Gordon W. Morrell, *Britain Confronts the Stalin Revolution: Anglo-Soviet Relations and the Metro-Vickers Crisis* (Waterloo, Canada: Wilfrid Laurier University Press, 1995), 182.

26. Michael Jabara Carley, *Silent Conflict: A Hidden History of Soviet-Western Relations* (Lanham, MD: Rowman & Littlefield, 2014), 326, 418.

27. Grigorii Zinoviev, "Rech na sobranii chlenov i kandidatov RKP Sokolnicheskogo raiona (29 sentiabria 1923 g.)," *Kommunisticheskaia revoliutsiia*, no. 17–18 (1923): 3–22 [here: 3]. We thank Gleb Albert for bringing this source to our attention.

final analysis, of course, coincide with the interests of the German and entire international proletariat."[28]

German revolutionary turmoil in 1923 fizzled and turned out to be the last ray of hope for an imminent revolution in Europe as well as a crushing disappointment to rank-and-file activists in the USSR.[29] Imminent or not, the Bolsheviks retained their faith in the world's revolutionary future and devoted more attention and resources to propaganda, training, and organizational work not only in Europe, but in other parts of the world as well. Again, they drew on Lenin's analysis of imperialism as the final stage of capitalism and on their own revolutionary experience: with sufficient effort and commitment the British and the French empires could meet the Russian Empire's fate, they believed.

In January 1924, Lenin died. Four main rivals—all old Bolsheviks—now vied more openly for power. A brilliant orator, military leader, organizer, and intellectual, Trotsky was the obvious contender. In fact, the others teamed up to thwart his rise. Zinoviev, the Party boss of Leningrad (as Petrograd was called after Lenin's death), had a strong power base in the old capital. Lev Kamenev (1883–1936) was acting chair of the Soviet government during Lenin's illness and Zinoviev's close ally. Both, despite their hesitancy in October 1917, were, like Trotsky, on the more radical wing of the Party. Nikolai Bukharin (1888–1938), a leading party intellectual and editor of the newspaper *Pravda*, was more moderate and an enthusiastic supporter of the New Economic Policy. Joseph Stalin (1879–1953), the Georgian-born Secretary General of the Party's Central Committee and the closest associate of Lenin, came out on top because of his control of patronage jobs in the Party, clever self-effacement during the struggles for power, and tactical brilliance. It also helped that in 1924, in part because of the failure of European revolution, he formulated an important foreign policy revision to Leninism, an idea encapsulated in the slogan "Socialism in One Country." Socialism, Stalin argued, could be built in Russia even if revolution never occurred in Europe. The USSR continued to promote

---

28. Zinoviev Report to the Central Committee, September 23, 1923, Russian State Archive of Socio-Political History (RGASPI), f. 17, op. 2, d. 101, ll. 4–13 ob., cited in G. M. Adibekov, Z. G. Adibekova, eds., *Politbiuro TsK RKP(b)-VKP(b) i Komintern: 1919–1943: Dokumenty* (Moscow: ROSSPEN, 2004), 187, 192, 194, 195.

29. See Gleb J. Albert, "'German October Is Approaching': Internationalism, Activists, and the Soviet State in 1923," *Revolutionary Russia* 24, no. 2 (December 2011), 111–42.

revolution worldwide but more than ever was seen by the Soviet leadership as its indispensable anchor state.

In the 1920s, the Bolsheviks opened four international schools within the USSR to educate and train revolutionaries from around the world. Two such schools opened in Moscow in the fall of 1921. While the Communist University of the National Minorities of the West catered to political activists from western Soviet regions as well as from countries of central and eastern Europe, the Communist University of the Toilers of the East opened its doors to students from the Soviet republics in Asia and to international students mostly from China, India, Indochina, and the Middle East (see Document 2.19). Four years later the University's Chinese Department was split off to give birth to the Sun Yat-sen University, which focused more specifically on activists from the Guomindang and the Chinese Communist Party. The following year the International Lenin School was instituted by the Comintern specifically for Communists from Europe and North America, as well as China. Thousands of students attended these schools, receiving ideological indoctrination and practical training in methods of revolutionary work. Many of them rose to positions of prominence in the worldwide revolutionary movement. The schools' alumni included such Communist Party leaders, statesmen, and heads of state as Iosip Broz Tito, Harry Haywood, Wladyslaw Gomulka, Erich Honecker, Nikolaos Zachariadis, Li Shaoqi, Deng Xiaoping, Ho Chi Minh, Khalid Bagdash, and Sen Katayama (see Map 6, p. 49). Perhaps the most emphatic manifestation of revolutionary interest in this period could be observed in the Bolsheviks' approach to China. Soon after seizing power, they abrogated the Russian Empire's unequal treaties signed with China after the crushing of the Boxer Rebellion (1899–1901). The Chinese Communist Party (CCP) was founded in 1920 and soon joined the Comintern.

Yet the Bolshevik leaders realized, and the Comintern's relationship with the CCP clearly showed, that promoting revolution abroad was an enormously complicated mission that required caution as well as boldness, awareness of changing social conditions, and political maneuvering of the highest caliber. In the course of the 1920s, the Bolshevik consensus was that the Chinese Communists were too weak for a Communist-led revolution and therefore had to work within a broader framework of the Guomindang— a revolutionary organization with a nationalist and anti-colonialist agenda headed by Chiang Kai-shek (1887–1975). The Bolsheviks actively supported the Guomindang, though only temporarily. As Stalin remarked on April 5, 1927, it had "to be utilized to the end, squeezed out like a lemon, and then flung away."[30] Yet Chiang Kai-shek refused to be "squeezed." In 1926–1927, Chiang's relations with the Communists soured as he consolidated his personal power. On April 18, 1927, he declared the creation of a separate government in Nanking, breaking ties with the left-leaning Guomindang government in Wuhan, a booming transportation and industrial hub in central China and a hotbed of communist activism. The Wuhan government had in turn grown increasingly hostile to the Communists because of their strong appeal and influence in the region. The splintering of the Guomindang thus created a real prospect for the political marginalization of the Chinese Communist Party. The Bolshevik leaders advised the Chinese Communists to remain tactically within the Wuhan government and allied to the Guomindang, while seeking to bring about a communist revolution (see Document 2.10). The Bolsheviks sent money, arms, and advisers. On December 10, 1927, the Politburo authorized a major uprising in Canton, but it failed, leading to waves of anticommunist repression. It then took the Chinese Communist Party two more decades to build itself into a formidable political and military force and to defeat the Guomindang in 1949.

As the revolutionary crisis in China unfolded, the Bolsheviks faced a security crisis in Europe. In May 1927, the police raided ARCOS's office in London, citing continued Soviet attempts to spy and promote revolution in Britain. The British government severed diplomatic relations with the USSR, triggering "the war scare" in Moscow. The Bolshevik response to the crises of 1927 was based on the interplay of revolutionary and state interests. On one hand, in 1928, the Comintern proclaimed that the post-revolutionary stabilization of capitalism had ended and that the "Third Period" of the development of capitalism would directly lead to its economic and revolutionary collapse. To many, this judgment seemed especially prescient after the onset of the Great Depression the following year. On the other hand, by the late 1920s the Comintern was firmly fused with the machinery of the Soviet state and worked closely with the Cheka's successor, the OGPU, and with military officials to advance

---

30. As quoted in Harold Isaacs, *The Tragedy of the Chinese Revolution*, 2d rev. ed. (Stanford, CA: Stanford University Press, 1961), 162.

Soviet state interests.[31] Survivability of the Soviet state and its readiness for war, defensive or revolutionary, was seen by Stalin and his supporters as more vital than ever and dictated rapid industrialization, agricultural modernization, militarization, political rigidity, and the destruction of enemies from within.

Not everyone agreed with Stalin's view of the Soviet state. Leon Trotsky and his allies worked hard to keep the revolutionary flame alive, claiming to be the true bearers of the Russian revolutionary legacy and goals. Expelled from the Soviet Union in 1929 as Stalin's archenemy, Trotsky along with his followers had tried at first to radicalize the Third International (Comintern) from within by forming the International Left Opposition. When that effort failed, Trotsky called for the creation of a Fourth International intended to mobilize workers and bring about a revolutionary transformation of the world amid the Great Depression, spread of fascist regimes, and increasing likelihood of a new world war (see Document 2.11).

Stalin saw Trotsky's approach as recklessly provocative and no less dangerous than fascism itself. By the mid-1930s, state interest and state security were paramount to Soviet foreign policy, as the Soviet state faced an existential threat potentially more dangerous than the German offensive of 1918 or the anti-Bolshevik offensives of the Civil War. Fully aware that Hitler viewed Russia as potential "living space" (*Lebensraum*) for the German people, the Soviet government was eager to meet the emerging threat of imperial conquest through a military buildup and robust state-interest-driven diplomacy, and was more than ever open to working with other states to create an international environment conducive to peace and stability in Europe. In 1932, the Soviet Union signed a non-aggression pact with Poland and, in 1934, finally joined the League of Nations. When the civil war broke out in Spain, Soviet support for the Spanish Republic's struggle against General Francisco Franco was motivated by concerns about the rise of fascism, not by revolutionary interest. A defensive Franco-Soviet Pact and a mutual assistance treaty with Czechoslovakia were reached in 1935, followed by frantic and ultimately unsuccessful attempts to

---

31. Top Comintern activists teamed up with leading Soviet military experts, including Vasilii Blukher and Mikhail Tukhachevskii, to produce a detailed analysis of successful strategies of revolutionary insurrection. The book was published in German in 1928 and in French in 1931, but only appeared in English in 1970. See A. Neuberg, *Armed Insurrection* (New York: St Martin's Press, 1970).

forge an Anglo-Franco-Soviet alliance against Hitler in 1939. Soviet diplomatic efforts notwithstanding, the cumulative impact of earlier revolutionary policies remained profound and resulted in intense and widely held suspicion about Soviet goals and intentions abroad.[32]

In the final analysis, the pursuit of the revolutionary interest in Soviet foreign policy during the interwar years exerted a powerful impact in Europe and beyond. Prodded by the Comintern, European Communists were animated by a nearly eschatological expectation of the "second coming" of the Russian Revolution. This attitude alienated the broader and more moderate left while re-energizing the right and the extreme right. Ultimately, revolutionary-interest-based Soviet policies failed to revolutionize Europe, but by eroding goodwill and trust in international relations, they contributed to the outbreak of another world war.

The Russian Revolution and the Power of Communism

The global power of the Russian Revolution cannot be fully grasped solely in terms of the destruction it wrought on one mighty empire, or of the Bolsheviks' organized efforts to transform Russia and globally spread the Russian revolutionary wave. As a source of both fear and hope, the Russian Revolution made a profound impact on people's hearts and minds worldwide. Indeed, the range of reactions around the world was truly dramatic. As the French communist journalist Pierre Pascal (1890–1983) put it: "Some, with more or less bad faith, insist on depicting a country of fire and blood, subjected to I don't know what gang of brigands, 'enemies of the human species,' wreaking only devastation, pillage, and murder. Others believe naïvely that the capitalist and bourgeois

---

32. A detailed discussion of the role of trust in the USSR can be found in Geoffrey Hosking (Guest Editor), "Trust and Distrust in the USSR," *Slavonic & East European Review*, Special Issue, vol. 91, no. 1 (2013). The critical role of distrust and suspicion towards the Soviet Union in Europe is discussed in R. H. Haigh, D. S. Morris, and A. R. Peters, *Soviet Foreign Policy, the League of Nations and Europe, 1917–1939* (Totowa, NJ: Barnes & Noble Books, 1986), 123–28. They nevertheless argue that aggressive ideology "tempered by *realpolitik*" defined Soviet foreign policy throughout the entire interwar period.

system are but a dim memory in Russia and that a perfect communist society has taken their place."[33]

Beyond intellectual debates and activities of professional revolutionaries lay the world of suffering and social tensions exacerbated by the calamities of the war that had just ended. Anger, resistance, and revolutionary turmoil broke out in both the devastated European imperial core and the colonial and semicolonial periphery. Map 6 shows a world in revolt, of which the Russian Revolution was an integral and critical element.[34]

This section will seek to convey the variety of ways in which people in many lands perceived and interpreted the Russian Revolution and to show—using selected examples among countless others—how these perceptions in turn affected their worldviews, pivotal choices, and actions. In broadest terms, responses to the Russian Revolution could be characterized as either hopeful or alarmist.

It can in fact be argued that Russian revolutionary ideas began to arouse global expectations even before revolution shattered the Russian Empire. A major industrialization drive of the 1890s gave Russia one of the fastest industrial growth rates in the world, and brought to life a burgeoning population of industrial workers and small armies of radical intellectuals passionately seeking to "revolutionize" them. Thousands of Russian revolutionaries were forced to escape Russia and used France, Britain, Switzerland, Germany, and the United States as safe havens for their underground work in Russia. This put them in close contact with their Western counterparts, especially the radical socialist minority that rejected the Great War. Equally important, hundreds of thousands of Russian industrial workers took part in the mass migration from Russia and eastern Europe to the United States. From 1881–1914, some three million Russian subjects (Russians, Jews, Poles, Ukrainians, etc.) made their home in America. There they encountered a much more developed industrial economy, in which the working conditions still left a lot to be desired. Russian-speaking activists championed the interests of American workers, attacking injustice and inequality. Such attacks resonated with many newcomers from eastern Europe.

---

33. Pierre Pascal, *En Russie rouge* (Paris: Édition de la Librairie de l'Humanité, 1921), 5.

34. This map is not comprehensive and does not imply direct causal connection with the Russian Revolution. It is meant to convey the context, scope, and diversity of contemporaneous revolutionary movements in the world.

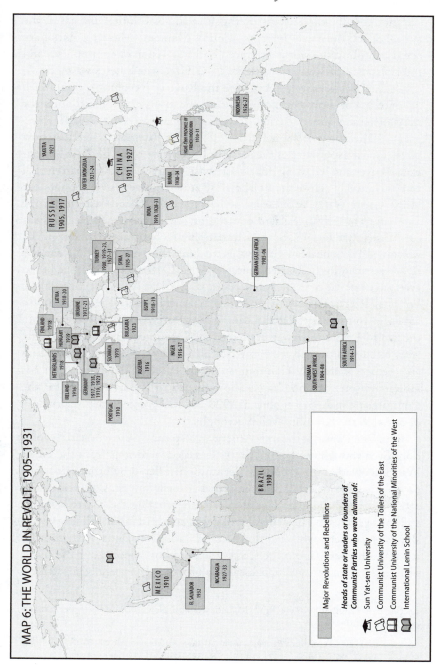

MAP 6: THE WORLD IN REVOLT, 1905–1931

YAKUTIA 1921

OUTER MONGOLIA 1921-24

RUSSIA 1905, 1917

CHINA 1911, 1927

BURMA 1930-34

INDONESIA 1926-27

NGHE-TINH PROVINCE OF FRENCH INDOCHINA 1930-31

INDIA 1919, 1928-31

TURKEY 1908, 1919-23, 1927-31

SYRIA 1925-27

GERMAN EAST AFRICA 1905-06

LATVIA 1918-20

UKRAINE 1917-21

EGYPT 1918-19

FINLAND 1918

HUNGARY 1919

BULGARIA 1923

NETHERLANDS 1918

SLOVAKIA 1919

NIGERIA 1916

NIGER 1916-17

SOUTH AFRICA 1914-15

IRELAND 1916

GERMANY 1917, 1918, 1919, 1923

GERMAN SOUTHWEST AFRICA 1904-08

PORTUGAL 1910

BRAZIL 1930

MEXICO 1910

EL SALVADOR 1932

NICARAGUA 1927-33

Major Revolutions and Rebellions

Heads of state or leaders or founders of Communist Parties who were alumni of:

Sun Yat-sen University

Communist University of the Toilers of the East

Communist University of the National Minorities of the West

International Lenin School

Undoubtedly, the success of the Russian Revolution increased the appeal of the Bolshevik interpretation of Marxism. Many revolutionary activists around the world embraced both the vision of communism and the Bolshevik pathway towards it. Their hope was buttressed by confidence that in a relatively short time the Russian Revolution would spill out into a world proletarian revolution and trigger a global communist transformation.

The experience of John Reed (1887–1920) demonstrates just how powerful the experience of the Russian Revolution could be.[35] An American reporter and left-wing political activist, he arrived in Russia in the fall of 1917, shortly before the Bolshevik seizure of power. A vocal opponent of the Great War, a year earlier he had traveled around eastern Europe and had observed war-related devastation and suffering. To Reed, it was capitalism that had made the catastrophic global war possible, and he welcomed the Bolsheviks' vision as, to him, the only viable alternative. Reed returned to the United States in April 1918, more radicalized than ever. In 1919, he actively participated in the Left Wing Section of the Socialist Party of America, accusing the Party's central leadership of a lack of revolutionary zeal and calling for greater worker involvement in the world revolutionary movement (see Document 3.1). Later in the year, Reed was purged from the Socialist Party's National Convention and helped found the Communist Labor Party of America. After his indictment on sedition charges, he returned to Russia to work for the Comintern. He died of typhus in 1920 and was granted the rare privilege of burial in the Kremlin Wall Necropolis.

John Reed was not the only American inspired by the Russian Revolution. Even though the United States emerged victorious from the Great War and avoided the economic devastation suffered by other victorious powers, it was not immune from growing social unrest. On February 6, 1919, a general strike broke out in Seattle, bringing the city to a standstill for five days.[36] The general strike was an act of labor solidarity with shipyard workers, who had downed their tools on January 21 in order to secure higher wages. The strike was not spontaneous, but the result of decisions made by union locals. It proceeded peacefully, as strikers

---

35. See Eric Homberger, *John Reed* (Manchester and New York: Manchester University Press, 1990).

36. See Harvey O'Connor, *Revolution in Seattle: A Memoir* (New York: Monthly Review Press, 1964), 90, 94, 102–3, 119, 158–59, 198–201, 210–11, 244.

sought to maintain core city services, as well as establish an alternative food distribution network. While the strike ended in an orderly fashion, the authorities' reaction to the strike was severe and involved arrests and the persecution of radical activists. To some of the strikers, the Russian Revolution served as an inspiring example (see Document 3.2).

Still, in the first years after the Russian Revolution its impact was the strongest in Europe. Strikes and uprisings rocked Germany, Hungary, Italy, and Spain, and Soviet-style soldier and worker councils made claims on political as well as economic power. As mentioned in the previous section, it seemed for a while that Germany was on the brink of a full-scale revolution. Among the revolutionaries who came closest to replicating the success of the Russian Revolution was Bela Kun (1886–1938).[37] A Hungarian Jew, Kun fought against the Russians in the Austro-Hungarian army and was captured as a prisoner of war. He joined the Bolshevik party organization in Tomsk, Siberia, and experienced the Russian Revolution firsthand. In early 1918, he moved to Petrograd and cofounded the Hungarian group of the Russian Communist Party. In November he left Russia for Hungary. No longer a part of the Austro-Hungarian Empire, Hungary was in the midst of severe economic, social, and political crises. On March 21, 1919, the Hungarian Soviet Republic was proclaimed, with Kun as Commissar for Foreign Affairs of the Revolutionary Governing Council. The Republic lasted for a mere 133 days before being crushed by Romanian forces. Kun returned to Russia with an unshaken belief in the global applicability of the Bolshevik revolutionary strategy (see Document 3.3).

Yet not all revolutionaries agreed to accept the Russian Revolution as a model to follow. Contrary to Bela Kun, Otto Rühle (1874–1943), a member of the radical German Spartacist League, argued that Bolshevik success in Russia, while admirable and important, could not be replicated in other countries due to its flawed emphasis on political coercion. To leftist radicals like Rühle, the Russian Revolution was a cautionary lesson of unjustified repression and state bureaucratization that set back the prospects of communism (see Document 3.4). In 1920, Rühle was among those who split from the German Communist Party (KPD), which they believed to be adhering too closely to the Bolshevik model, in order to form an independent Communist Workers' Party of Germany

---

37. See Gyorgy Borsanyi, *The Life of a Communist Revolutionary: Bela Kun* (Boulder, CO: Social Science Monographs, 1993).

(KAPD). The following year, the KAPD left the Comintern and eventually splintered into smaller communist groups.[38]

The Russian Revolution appealed not just to professional revolutionaries. Many intellectuals believed that capitalism, especially after the Great War, was irredeemable not only on economic, but on moral grounds. They admired the Russian Revolution's anti-capitalist and anti-nationalist fervor but had reservations about where it stood in relation to humanistic values and freedom. When the French Communist novelist Henri Barbusse (1873–1935) accused left-leaning intellectuals of trying to stay above the fray instead of joining the cause of the communist revolution, Romain Rolland (1866–1944), a Nobel-Prize-winning French author, responded with a sympathetic, but cautious rejoinder (see Document 3.5). A lively intellectual debate followed, drawing contributions from over forty writers and publicists from France, Germany, Switzerland, and Italy. The debate centered on issues of social struggle and violence, but also on the meaning of individual autonomy and intellectual freedom.[39]

Like Barbusse, the Russian-born American anarchist Emma Goldman (1869–1940), hailed the Russian Revolution and the Bolsheviks. Deported back to Russia in 1919 by American officials for radical activity, she soon discovered many of the same problems that concerned Rolland. It took her a year to come to terms with what she observed. Revolutionary Russia, as it turned out, was now a Bolshevik state, intolerant of individual freedoms and political dissent. Goldman was particularly shocked by the brutal government suppression of worker strikes and the Kronstadt sailor rebellion in 1921. She left Russia later that year (see Document 3.6).

Goldman's deportation from the United States took place in the heat of the "First Red Scare"—a brief but intense period of anticommunist fears and paranoia that affected the American public sphere as well as various government agencies in the wake of the Russian Revolution. In November 1919 and January 1920, US Attorney General A. Mitchell Palmer (1872–1936) initiated raids resulting in the arrest of thousands and the deportation of hundreds of suspected radicals, often without due process. The Red Scare subsided after Palmer's stern warning of an imminent revolution in May 1920 failed to materialize. It nevertheless had a lasting

---

38. See Pierre Broué, *The German Revolution, 1917–1923*, trans. John Archer, ed. Ian Birchall and Brian Pearce (Chicago: Haymarket Books, 2006).

39. David James Fischer, *Romain Rolland and the Politics of International Engagement* (Berkley, Los Angeles, and Oxford: University of California Press, 1988), 80–111.

impact on American political and public life by forging a rigid ideological conception of "Americanism" and branding a variety of radical views and activities as "un-American." The cartoon in Figure 14 captures the fears of those who believed that the Russian Revolution was a threat to civilization, a development ridden with chaos, violence, and devastation.

Admittedly, the Russian Revolution did not by itself cause the Red Scare; other forces had also been at work. For nearly three decades, rapid industrialization and waves of immigration from eastern and central Europe had challenged the widely cherished myth of a homogenous, individualistic, and harmonious American society, and had given rise to a growing suspicion and resentment toward foreign radicals, and even immigrants more broadly. But the spectacular success of the Russian Revolution, the postwar resurgence of the labor movement, and anarchist bomb attacks turned this resentment into fear. Furthermore, the defeat of the Central Powers, whose leaders had often been portrayed by wartime propaganda as barbaric and a danger to "civilization," left an empty niche in many people's minds that was quickly filled by perceptions of

Figure 14: "Put Them Out and Keep Them Out" (1919)

pro-Bolshevik activists who seemed to care more about socialist revolution than about America. Revolutionary subversion became a convenient explanation for a host of America's postwar ills.

The fear of the Russian Revolution was even stronger in Europe. European political elites were alarmed about the Bolsheviks' revolutionary policies and domestic social unrest because many countries in postwar Europe seemed just as susceptible to revolution as the Russian Empire had been. When in 1919 Woodrow Wilson and David Lloyd George contemplated involving Soviet Russia in the Paris Peace Conference, called by victorious powers to set peace terms for Germany and its allies they realized that they could count on support from neither one of the other conference participants (particularly French Prime Minister Georges Clemenceau), "nor the public opinion of our countries which was frightened by Bolshevik violence and feared its spread," as Lloyd

George later admitted.[40] In fact, some, like Danish diplomat and soon-to-be foreign minister Harald Scavenius, voiced alarm about the spread of Bolshevism to Germany and called for its speedy destruction by military means (see Document 3.7). There was, however, little appetite in Europe for such a far-reaching military campaign. A key, but understandable, result of the Bolshevik Revolution was to exclude Russia from the postwar settlement negotiations, which weakened the emerging interwar security system and probably made it easier for Hitler to pursue his vision of world domination.[41]

More than any other event, the Russian Revolution, along with Germany's defeat in World War I, shaped Adolf Hitler's worldview.[42] He drew three principal lessons from it. First, its evolution underscored the critical role of oral propaganda for stirring and leading the masses. Second, Hitler concluded that in order for his movement to be effective, it had to offer not just specific policy solutions, but an inspiring vision of the future. Finally, he saw in the Russian Empire a country and a culture that was crushed first and foremost by Jews in Bolshevik attire. To Hitler, the Russian Revolution was proof that Germany could suffer the same fate, unless the German people rose to resist communist propaganda. At the same time, he was profoundly skeptical about the stability and viability of "Jewish-dominated" Soviet Russia. In Hitler's view, Russia's "rotten structure" of governance made it an appealing target for German conquest and colonization, a unique opportunity to turn Germany into a vast continental power on par with the British Empire and the United States (see Document 3.8).

The revolutionary collapse of the Russian Empire together with the rising appeal of internationalist communist ideals and activism served as a rallying point for extreme nationalist and fascist groups across the European continent, facilitating their rise to power first in Italy, then in central Europe, and finally in Germany and in Spain.

While Great Britain's liberal democracy survived, British politics were not immune to fears inspired by the Russian Revolution. On October 8, 1924, a vote of no confidence in the House of Commons brought down

---

40. See Stephen M. Walt, *Revolution and War* (Ithaca and London: Cornell University Press, 1996), 161–62 (quotation: 162n105).

41. See Dominic Lieven, *Towards the Flame: Empire, War and the End of Tsarist Russia* (London: Allen Lane, 2015) 362–64.

42. See Eugene Davidson, *The Making of Adolf Hitler: The Birth and Rise of Nazism*, 1st University of Missouri Press pbk. ed. (Columbia: University of Missouri Press, 1997), 101–18.

the first Labor government in British history. Formed in January by Prime Minister Ramsay MacDonald (1866–1937), it had been under fire for restoring diplomatic relations with the USSR, signing the Anglo-Soviet Trade Agreement, and most immediately for refusing to prosecute a communist editor for incitement to mutiny. A major political scandal broke out when just days before the election the *Daily Mail* published a letter supposedly written by the Chairman of the Comintern, Grigorii Zinoviev, to the British Communist Party urging it to engage in subversive activities (see Document 3.9). The letter became a welcome propaganda gift to the opposition, as shown in Figure 15. Historians debate whether the letter actually helped to tip the electoral scales in favor of the Conservatives, though they agree it was a forgery. As such, the letter sheds light not on Comintern activities in Britain, but on ways in which perceptions and fears of revolutionary communism affected British politics and public discourse.

In the following decade, as Stalin pursued rapid industrialization and collectivization and used brutal force to destroy his real and imagined enemies, many Europeans continued to perceive Soviet Russia and the revolutionary appeal of communism as an equal, if not greater, threat to international stability and security than Nazism and fascism. One of these many was Neville Chamberlain (1869–1940), whose views and actions proved pivotal to European security, when he served as British Prime Minister from May 1937 to May 1940. Chamberlain viewed even the February Revolution skeptically. To him, it was a manifestation of a revolutionary ferment "in all the unsteady brains of the world," which could only hurt, not help, the war cause. From the first weeks of the Bolshevik seizure of power, he believed the Revolution had plunged Russia into chaos. His only consolation was that this catastrophe would sober up revolutionaries in other countries: "If the Russian Revolution had been a success instead of a complete disaster, it would have had a very deep and ugly reverberation over here." Like most members of the British conservative political establishment, he was deeply concerned with Soviet attempts to finance, infiltrate, and influence the British labor movement and radical left. Like most, he did not doubt the authenticity of the forged "Zinoviev letter."[43] The British general strike in May 1926

---

43. Keith Feiling, *The Life of Neville Chamberlain* (London: MacMillan, 1970), 79–80 ("unsteady brains"); Robert Self, *Neville Chamberlain: A Biography* (London and Burlington, VT: Ashgate, 2006), 366; Robert Self, ed., *The Neville Chamberlain Diary Letters* (Aldershot, Burlington, Singapore, and Sydney: Ashgate, 2000), 1:234–235, 257 ("ugly reverberation"), 320, 323; 2:133, 305, 353; 3:356.

ON THE LOAN TRAIL.

[In a document just disclosed by the British Foreign Office (apparently after considerable delay), M. ZINOVIEFF, a member of the Bolshevist Dictatorship, urges the British Communist Party to use "the greatest possible energy" in securing the ratification of Mr. MACDONALD's Anglo-Russian Treaty, in order to facilitate a scheme for "an armed insurrection" of the British proletariat.]

Figure 15: "Vote for MacDonald and Me" (*Punch* magazine, 1924)

only reinforced suspicions and fears of Soviet involvement as the Politburo channeled funds to the strikers and the Comintern gave orders to the British Communist Party to politicize the strike and bring down the Conservative government. Chamberlain's "diary letters" to his sisters (see Document 3.10) confirm that his unease about "the Bolshies" persisted throughout the 1930s. Despite pressure from opposition leaders and some fellow Conservatives like Winston Churchill (1874–1965), Chamberlain remained deeply skeptical about drawing closer to the Bolsheviks, thus making the forging of an Anglo-Franco-Soviet military alliance against Hitler in 1939 unlikely and ultimately impossible.

Chamberlain was not alone in his skepticism. Profound suspicion of Soviet Russia pervaded the East European capitals. Their governing elites had directly experienced the Russian Revolution and saw their countries as continuously threatened by it. In 1938, the "barrier policy" of Poland and Romania made any Soviet assistance to Czechoslovakia unfeasible. In 1939 the Baltic states refused to enter into any security agreement with the USSR that would allow Soviet military intervention. Poland, mindful of the Soviet revolutionary goals in the Polish-Soviet War of 1920 and fearful of losing its eastern provinces, refused point blank to grant Soviet troops the right of transit through the Polish territory, even for the purpose of rebuffing the Germans. This, to borrow a term William Irvine applied to French conservative politics,[44] was a "war-revolution nexus": a belief that a military conflict, particularly with Soviet involvement, could morph into revolutionary turmoil. This belief was rooted in an ideological rejection of communism, in an apprehension about Soviet foreign policy goals, but also in the historical memory of the Russian Revolution.

British unease about Soviet Russia was rooted not just in history, but in the realization that the British Empire was even more globally extended and diverse than the Russian Empire had been, and therefore potentially even more vulnerable to revolutionary unrest. Indeed, the Russian Revolution impressed many anti-colonial activists fighting against British imperial domination of their countries and lands. The ardent commitment of Jawaharlal Nehru (1889–1964) to India's freedom can be traced to his early years. Born in India, Nehru studied in Britain before returning home to practice law and pursue a nationalist political agenda. A cosmopolitan background made Nehru attuned to the international dimensions of India's struggle for self-rule and eventual independence. He was encouraged by the Boer War (1899–1902), which challenged British dominance in South Africa, as well as by the

---

44. As quoted in Michael Jabara Carley, *1939: The Alliance that Never Was and the Coming of World War II* (Chicago: I. R. Dee, 1999), xv. One could argue that the Bolsheviks embraced the reverse version of this nexus, expecting revolutionary turmoil to spark a war with Soviet Russia's involvement.

Russo-Japanese War (1904–1905), which triggered the Russian Revolution of 1905. The cataclysm of the Great War and the collapse of the Russian Empire in 1917 filled him with optimism about India's prospects for breaking free from the British Empire (see Document 3.11). Marxism helped Nehru to develop a universal conceptual framework of change, in which India's struggle against British rule was but one example of the world's transition from capitalism to a superior social order. He was not alone in this thinking, for, in his words, "The younger men and women of the [Indian National] Congress, who used to read Bryce on Democracies[45] and Motley[46] and Keith[47] and Mazzini,[48] were now reading, when they could get them, books on socialism and communism and Russia."[49] Nehru's optimism, patience, and perseverance ultimately bore fruit. He became the first prime minister of an independent India in 1947, after thirty-five years of engagement in anti-colonial struggle and politics.

An awareness of the Russian Revolution's significance for anti-colonial struggle spread throughout the developing world, though it took time for many activists to realize its potential and appeal. Josiah Tshangana Gumede (1867–1946) was a black Christian of Zulu ancestry and a founding member of the South African Native National Congress, renamed the African National Congress (ANC) in 1923. Despite his earlier opposition to Bolshevism, Gumede realized that building international support could revitalize the ANC, whose mass following declined in the 1920s. Gumede agreed to participate in the Founding Congress of the Comintern-sponsored League Against Imperialism, which took place in 1927 in Brussels. Later in the year, as president general of the ANC, Gumede journeyed to the Soviet Union to take part in the celebration of the tenth anniversary of the October Revolution. He visited Moscow and then traveled around the Soviet Republic of Georgia. The experience

---

45. James Bryce (1838–1922), a British academic and statesman, published *Modern Democracies*, 2 vols. (1921).

46. Probably John Lothrop Motley (1814–1877), an American, who authored *Historic Progress and American Democracy* (1868).

47. Arthur Berriedale Keith (1879–1944) was a Scottish scholar of Sanskrit and constitutional law. He authored *The Constitutional Law of the British Dominions* (1933) and *A Constitutional History of India, 1600–1935* (1936), among other works.

48. Giuseppe Mazzini (1805–1872) fought for Italian unification.

49. Jawaharlal Nehru, *An Autobiography with Musings on Recent Events in India* (London: John Lane, 1936), 364.

was overwhelming. The Communists he met stood against racism and accepted him as an equal. The post-revolutionary social order in Russia appeared equally color-blind. As he solemnly declared upon his return to South Africa, "I have been to the New Jerusalem....I have brought a key [that will] unlock the door to freedom."[50] Gumede concluded that the Communists were allies in the black South Africans' struggle against British domination and racial injustice, and that their struggle was part of a global fight against imperialism (see Document 3.12). Gumede proposed a strategy of closer cooperation with the Communists, "the only people who are with us in spirit." His strategy met with resistance from the more moderate activists in the ANC, as well as from some tribal leaders who pointed out that the Bolsheviks had killed the tsar of Russia and were no friends to tribal hierarchies. Even though Gumede failed to gain immediate support for his agenda in the 1930s, after World War II the ANC did grow into a mass-based organization that forged an alliance with the South African Communist Party and has dominated post-apartheid politics.

Many African-American radical activists promptly welcomed the Russian Revolution, including the socialist editors of a leading African-American magazine, the *Messenger*, A. Philip Randolph (1889–1979) and Chandler Owen (1889–1967). W. E. B. Du Bois (1868–1963), a co-founder of the National Association for the Advancement of Colored People (NAACP), was at first skeptical of communism. An African-American scholar, writer, and civil rights activist, Du Bois believed that the cause of racial equality was broader than the dictates of any particular ideology. Yet witnessing entrenched, violent racism in America—for example the widespread attacks on blacks during the Red Scare in the "Red Summer" of 1919—outraged him. Then in 1926 he visited the Soviet Union for two months. What he saw convinced him definitively that racism was not just America's national disgrace, but also an essential by-product of global capitalism. The Russian Revolution, he concluded, offered an alternative to capitalism and therefore to racism. Shortly after his return to the United States, Du Bois published several articles detailing his observations and thoughts about Soviet Russia, in which he argued that socialism was a fair and just social order that could do away with racial, as well as class, inequality and oppression (see Document

---

50. "African National Congress Welcomes Gumede," *South African Worker*, vol. 12 (March 2, 1928), 2.

3.13). He ultimately concluded that the Russian Revolution was more profound than even the French Revolution and called the Soviet Union the "most hopeful country on earth." Du Bois continued to disagree with American Communists on issues of political strategy, criticized Joseph Stalin's tyrannical rule, and joined the Communist Party only in 1961 (largely to protest specific repressive policies of the US government). But his belief that socialism was capable of transforming human nature itself only grew stronger with the decades and resonated well beyond the NAACP.[51]

Although the Bolsheviks at first paid scant attention to Latin America, the inspirational impact of the Russian Revolution could be observed across the continent. It appealed to those who sought a radical solution to rural poverty, participated in the struggles of a small but growing industrial worker class, or attacked the entrenched social and cultural conservatism of the landed elites, especially as the concurrent revolution in Mexico (1910–1920) stopped short of completely transforming society. This sentiment was aptly summed up by an Argentinian scholar and activist José Ingenieros (1877–1925), who, speaking at a mass rally in Buenos Aires in November 1918, declared that "for those who view the course of history with a panoramic vision that ignores the trivial, the Russian Revolution marks the arrival of social justice in the world."[52]

In Chile, the Russian Revolution convinced worker activist and the founder of the Socialist Worker's Party, Luis Emilio Recabarren (1876–1924), that the Bolsheviks offered the right model of evolutionary transformation and in 1922 he spearheaded his party's transformation into a Communist Party and a member of the Comintern.

José Carlos Mariátegui (1894–1930) was a Peruvian political thinker, journalist, newspaper editor, and Marxist activist. In 1919, given his strident left-wing political stance, the Peruvian government arranged to send him abroad. He traveled and lived in Europe until 1923 and came back with a firm belief that what started in Russia was a world revolution,

---

51. See Gerald Horne and Mary Young, eds., *W. E. B. Du Bois: An Encyclopedia* (Westport, CT and London: Greenwood Press, 2001), 187–89, 195–98; David L. Lewis, *W. E. B. Du Bois, a Biography* (New York: Henry Holt and Co., 2009), 386, 486–87, 553, 669 (quotation: 669).

52. As recounted by Anibal Ponce, *Jose Ingenieros, su vida y su obra, 1926* in *Obras Completas* (Buenos Aires: Ed. Hector Matera, 1957), 88–90, cited in Michael Lowy, ed. *Marxism in Latin America from 1909 to the Present: An Anthology* (New Jersey and London: Humanities Press, 1992), 21.

bound to engulf other continents. He welcomed the Comintern's reach to Asia (see Document 3.14) and eventually to Latin America, but later on criticized the Comintern's narrow focus on Peruvian workers at the expense of the overwhelming peasant majority. One of the most original Marxist thinkers in Latin America, Mariátegui viewed the struggles of Peruvian peasants and indigenous people as part of a global revolutionary change.

In Puerto Rico, Dr. José Lanauze Rolón helped establish the Birth Control League of Puerto Rico, but was met with fierce opposition from the Catholic Church. Not a Communist at first, Rolón grew increasingly interested in the Russian Revolution's overthrow of the entire social and political order (see Document 3.15). In 1934, he became a founding member of the Puerto Rican Communist Party.

The country outside Europe where the Russian Revolution had the biggest impact was China. Then in his twenties, Mao Zedong (1893–1976) advocated China's modernization and supported the principles of republican government. Mao became an adamant supporter of Sun Yat-sen (1866–1925), the first president of the Republic of China, which emerged amid the Revolution of 1911 and the collapse of the Qing Dynasty. At that time, Mao was aware of communist ideas, but was not in a rush to embrace them. His shift in attitude took place as China's republican government failed to bring order and stability to the country, while the living conditions of China's peasants and workers remained abysmal. As an assistant librarian at Peking University, Mao read avidly about the Bolsheviks, their policies, and ideology. The Bolshevik view of the Great War as fundamentally imperialist made all the more sense to Mao as the Versailles Conference had handed control of China's northeastern Shandong Province from Germany to Japan. To Chinese patriots there could be no greater hypocrisy, no greater contrast between the democratic rhetoric of the victorious powers and reality. Echoing the views of one of the founders of the Communist Party of China (the CPC), Li Dazhao (1888–1927), Mao wrote in 1921 that "absolute liberalism, anarchism, even democracy" were fine in theory, but not in practice. The communist revolution in predominantly rural Russia, on the other hand, seemed to offer an immediate and practical recipe for China's woes.[53] Later that year, Mao became one of the thirteen delegates to the First National Congress of the CPC.

---

53. See A. Pantsov, *The Bolsheviks and the Chinese Revolution, 1919–1927* (Honolulu: University of Hawaii Press, 2000).

He was not the only one to be impressed by the Russian Revolution. As one Communist activist later put it, "Until the Chinese learned about the Russian Revolution, we were no good at politics and we made fools of ourselves. However, now the Chinese Communists have learned from the Russians how to have a revolution and no one laughs any more about the Chinese revolution."[54] It took Chinese Communists twenty-eight years of struggle against regional warlords, Japanese forces, and rival nationalists to come to power on a revolutionary wave that first rose in Russia in 1917 (see Document 3.16).

In the course of the two decades following the Russian Revolution, its impact reached all corners of the world touching the hearts and minds of millions of people. In the second half of the twentieth century, the mystique of the Russian Revolution began to fade as its main progeny, the Soviet Union, grew increasingly ossified and then collapsed under the pressure of economic, political, and nationalist forces it could no longer suppress or contain. Both the hopes and fears inspired by the Russian Revolution no longer haunt the developed or the developing world. The Russian Revolution powerfully impacted world history in the twentieth century, but does its influence extend to the present? As the Epilogue suggests, shock waves of the Russian Revolution continue to reverberate even in contemporary Eurasian geopolitics.

A Historiographical Note

The ripple effects of the Russian Revolution assumed many forms and lasted for decades. It took time for mature scholarly analysis to develop as well. By mid-century, the Soviet Union appeared at the peak of its power and influence, which encouraged scholars to look at the Russian Revolution as a source of the Soviet Union's success. To E. H. Carr, the British author of a multi-volume study of Soviet Russia—the first three volumes of which were devoted to the Russian Revolution (1950–1953)—it marked a new era in history, in which the value of individuals and liberal ideas diminished, perhaps irrevocably. While Carr downplayed the effectiveness of the deliberate global outreach by the Bolsheviks, he pointed to the tremendous anti-capitalist appeal of the Russian Revolution in the

---

54. Quoted in David Priestland, *The Red Flag: Communism and the Making of the Modern World* (London: Allen Lane, 2009), 264–65.

developing world. Most importantly, he argued that despite violence and brutality, the Revolution led to the creation of a powerful new state, a new system of social and political organization, and a new pathway toward modernization.

A more skeptical view was advanced by Arnold J. Toynbee (1967), who noted that the success of the Soviet Union paled in comparison to the initial worldwide expectations of the Bolsheviks and their supporters. The "myth" of the communist future gradually lost its exhilarating appeal, and nationalism and the major historic religions ultimately proved more potent in captivating people's minds. Even European Communists drifted further away from the violent revolutionary tradition. Toynbee believed that Western political culture was by and large not receptive to Bolshevik radicalism. He concluded, surprisingly, that the Russian Revolution's greatest impact came from its reorientation of the United States from a revolutionary into a conservative power.

In a somewhat similar vein, a group of French historians, including Victor Fay, Marc Ferro, and Pierre Broué, sought to examine why the revolution in Russia failed to precipitate other successful revolutions in Eastern, Central, and Western Europe (1967). They concluded that the rest of Europe simply had not experienced economic, social, and political crises of similar severity. Public opinion in France had been intensely focused on not losing the Great War; nationalist agendas had remained strong in the collapsing multinational empires of central and eastern Europe; the extreme left in Germany, Italy, and Austria remained marginalized; and even in Hungary, where a Soviet republic was briefly established, the revolutionaries failed to pursue balanced policies towards the peasantry and lacked the clandestine experience and structure of the Bolshevik party to maintain their grip on power. Moreover, the French historians viewed the Russian Revolution's failure to spread globally as a key reason for the increase in government coercion and repressiveness under Stalin.

Of course, as Eric Hobsbawm later pointed out, Lenin's model of centralized and coercive party organization proved extraordinarily effective in non-Western countries (1995). Within thirty to forty years, one-third of humanity was living under a regime derived from the Russian Revolution. Hobsbawm also viewed the impact of the Russian Revolution in Western countries far more favorably than Toynbee. It proved to be "the savior of liberal capitalism," he argued, by helping the West to win the war against Nazi Germany and by providing incentives for reform and accommodation of some moderate socialist demands.

Implicit in these arguments about the limits and failures of the Russian Revolution was the view that it was a specifically Russian phenomenon, not easily replicable in other countries or cultures, especially Western ones. By contrast, Paul Dukes mapped out the impact of the Russian Revolution on people's minds around the world, from Germany to Polynesia (1979). Dukes focused exclusively on the first five postrevolutionary years and mostly on sympathetic observers. Even so, he concluded that the Russian Revolution "belonged to the whole world." While it failed to meet the expectations of most of its supporters, so did the English, American, and French Revolutions. The very fact that it offered mankind "a rising cause," he reasoned, was far more historically significant than any specific failures.

Comparative studies of revolutions in the modern world worked in the same direction. Several historians and sociologists, in particular Crane Brinton (1965), Theda Skocpol (1979), Bailey Stone (2014), and Jack Goldstone (2014), who have examined the Russian Revolution in a comparative perspective, developed elaborate typologies of modern revolutions. Such an approach helped conceive of the Russian Revolution as both a global phenomenon and one of many revolutions during the past century.

Along similar lines, Mark N. Katz has focused on how revolutions have disrupted international order (1997). He conceptualized twentieth-century revolutions as forming "revolutionary waves," of which the first was Russia's "Marxist-Leninist wave." Many others have followed, including the struggle against colonialism and more recently "Arab nationalist" and "Islamic fundamentalist" waves.

In a posthumously published work, Martin Malia interpreted the Russian Revolution as one of many uniquely European revolutions, which extended across the world along with the projection of Europe's power and influence, intellectual as well as economic (2006). The reason why Marxist ideology, which emphasized the revolutionary agency of industrial workers, turned out to be most successful in predominantly agrarian societies was because Marxism originally grew out of Europe's pre-industrial periphery (1840s Germany) and provided ready, albeit fundamentally defective, recipes for swift development by revolutionary means. This made Marxism appealing to people in countries politically and economically backward compared to Western Europe. Thus the Russian Revolution served as a springboard for projecting European notions of modernity, progress, and change onto the wider world. Malia's final assessment of the Russian Revolution, however, was deeply negative, because of the lack of a positive legacy and the catastrophic human toll. Peter Holquist provides a clue to the Bolsheviks' resort to extraordinary violence and coercion (2002). In his interpretation, Western Europe did not only contribute ideas to this outcome but also provided the context of total mobilization during the First World War, out of which the Bolshevik revolutionary experience emerged.

Failure or not, according to Michael Richards, in terms of significance, the Russian Revolution "set the standard for revolution in the twentieth century, just as the French Revolution had done for the nineteenth century" (2004). The Russian Revolution resulted not only in the creation of a new major power—the Soviet Union—but also elicited numerous actions and policy responses from countries not directly affected by it. Most important, after the Russian Revolution and in part because of it, no other revolution could occur in isolation.

Epilogue

Eurasia's current distribution of political power and state borders—and the ethnic, religious, national, and cultural identities and conflicts that surround them—are to a significant degree products of the Russian Revolution. For decades, the destructive force of the Revolution, which led to the collapse of the Russian Empire, had been overshadowed by its constructive legacy—the birth of a new state and the building of a new Soviet Empire based on markedly different principles of administrative organization, social and ethnic integration, and control. The failure and collapse of that construction draw attention again to the profundity and intensity of the Revolution's original destructive impulses. A hundred years later, the disintegration of the Russian Empire appears to have been no less historically significant than the rise and fall of the Soviet Union. Not only was this the first European imperial collapse, which was followed by the downfall of the Austro-Hungarian and German (and later British, French, Belgian, Dutch, and Portuguese) empires, but the reverberations of that collapse continue to this day and invite the reconceptualization of the "post-Soviet space" as a "post-Imperial space."

When viewed against the backdrop of the vanished Russian imperial borders and internal administrative divisions, Map 7 reveals some twenty new post-Imperial states that emerged out of the revolutionary cataclysm

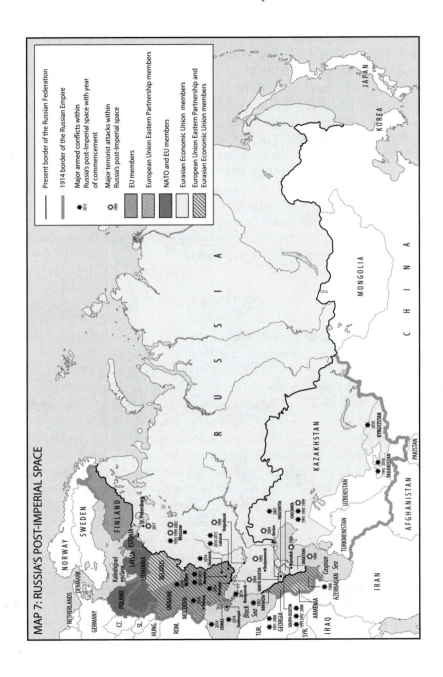

MAP 7: RUSSIA'S POST-IMPERIAL SPACE

of 1917. Some were quickly absorbed by the Bolshevik-designed Soviet Union, yet re-emerged again in the wake of its shattering in 1991 and their fates since have differed substantially. To complicate matters, these post-revolutionary state borders have rarely matched the boundaries of conflicted and conflicting ethnic and cultural identities.

Russia's "post-Imperial space" also has visionary dimensions, which give insight into the present thinking and agenda of the Putin-led Russian government. One of the questions in the public debate about Putin's intentions and goals is whether he is bent on rebuilding the Soviet Union. Such an outcome, however, would require a degree of ideological and doctrinal cohesiveness in Russian foreign policy that it has lacked in the post-Soviet era. Putin's actions bear the mark of spontaneity and often appear to be responses to short-term challenges, not part of a single grand design. It may be more productive to think about Putin's foreign policy in Eurasia as broadly geared towards a conversion of "the post-Imperial space" into a "neo-Imperial space." "Neo-Imperial space" is not tantamount to the rebuilding of either the Soviet Union, or of the Russian Empire, for which Russia clearly lacks the resources and will. It would, however, allow Russia to pursue escalating influence, dominance, and control over its neighbors. Even as several former parts of the Russian Empire are now members of the European Union and NATO, as Map 7 shows, Russia is vigorously pursuing its own version of economic and political integration by forging and taking the lead in the Eurasian Economic Union, which at present includes Belarus, Kazakhstan, Kyrgyzstan, and Armenia. None of these countries are stable democracies. Their attempts to simultaneously pursue integration with the European Union were abandoned or curtailed under pressure from the Putin government. Two other post-Imperial states, Moldova and particularly Ukraine, were forcefully, yet so far unsuccessfully, pressured to slow down or abandon rapprochement with the European Union. The territorial integrity of two post-Imperial states—Ukraine and Georgia—remains compromised as a result of Russia's recent military actions.

Such tactics, along with myriad other economic, political, military, and propaganda measures help project Russia's power in the post-Imperial space. In addition, in recent years the Putin government has begun to exert political, economic, and propagandistic influence on a global scale, providing financial support to extremist groups in Europe, offering enticing deals to friendly businesses and politicians, meddling in the democratic process in Western countries, and building an international propaganda network that now reaches all continents. Even though this effort to project power is far feebler than that of the Bolsheviks, and lacks any ideological coherence, it indicates that in historical terms Putin is trying to present himself as a bearer of the great power traditions of both Imperial and Soviet Russia. How much violence and aggression he is prepared (or allowed) to commit to achieve his goals remains an open question to this day.

DOCUMENTS

Section 1
Russia's Revolutions: From the Collapse of the Monarchy to the Civil War

1.1
Konstantin Pobedonostsev Blasts Parliamentarism, the Free Press, and Modern Education[1]

While Nicholas II seldom articulated his political beliefs, the following excerpts from an article by his tutor, Konstantin Pobedonostsev (1827–1907), a leading statesman, sheds light on his thinking about autocracy as a system of government far superior to parliamentary democracy and other modern European institutions. The theme of Russia's political and cultural superiority, on which Pobedonostsev dwells, persisted through the revolutionary era and managed to outlive it.

The New Democracy

What is this *freedom* by which so many minds are agitated, which inspires so many insensate actions, so many wild speeches, which leads the people so often to misfortune?...In a Democracy, the real rulers are the dexterous manipulators of votes, with their henchmen, the mechanics who so skillfully operate the hidden springs which move the puppets in the

---

1. Source: K. P. Pobedonostsev, *Moskovskii sbornik*, 2d ed. (Moscow: Sinodal'naia tipografiia, 1896), 25–27, 57–58, 60–61, 69–70.

arena of democratic elections. Men of this kind are ever ready with loud speeches lauding equality; in reality, they rule the people as any despot or military dictator might rule it.... The history of mankind bears witness that the most necessary and fruitful reforms—the most durable measures—emanated from the supreme will of statesmen, or from a minority enlightened by lofty ideas and deep knowledge, and that, on the contrary, the extension of the representative principle is accompanied by an abasement of political ideas and the vulgarization of opinions in the mass of the electors...

This is how the representative principle works in practice. The ambitious man comes before his fellow-citizens, and strives by every means to convince them that he more than any other is worthy of their confidence. What motives impel him to this quest? It is hard to believe that he is impelled by disinterested zeal for the public good....

The Press

...the journalist with a power comprehending all things, requires no sanction. He derives his authority from no election, he receives support from no one. His newspaper becomes an authority in the State, and for this authority no endorsement is required. The man in the street may establish such an organ and exercise the concomitant authority with an irresponsibility enjoyed by no other power in the world. That this is in no way exaggeration there are innumerable proofs. How often have superficial and unscrupulous journalists paved the way for revolution, fomented irritation into enmity, and brought about desolating wars! For conduct such as this a monarch would lose his throne, a minister would be disgraced, impeached, and punished; but the journalist stands dry above the waters he has disturbed, from the ruin he has caused he rises triumphant, and briskly continues his destructive work.

On Education

But infinite evil has been wrought by the prevalent confusion of knowledge and power. Seduced by the fantasy of universal enlightenment, we confuse education with a certain sum of knowledge acquired by completing the courses of schools, skillfully elaborated in the studies of pedagogues. Having organized our school thus, we isolate it from life, and secure by force the attendance of children whom we subject to a process of intellectual training in accordance with our program. But we ignore or forget that the mass of the children whom we educate must earn their daily bread, a labor for which the abstract notions on which our programs are constructed will be vain; while in the interests of some imaginary knowledge we withhold that training in productive labor which alone will bear fruit. Such are the results of our complex educational system, and such are the causes of the aversion with which the masses regard our schools, for which they can find no use.

* * *

Yet we waste our time discussing courses for elementary schools and obligatory programs which are to be the bases of a finished education. One would include an encyclopedic instruction;…another insists on the necessity for the agriculturist to know physics, chemistry, agricultural economy, and medicine; while a third demands a course of political economy and jurisprudence. But few reflect that by tearing the child from the domestic hearth for such a lofty destiny, they deprive his parents of a productive force which is essential to the maintenance of the home, while by raising before his eyes the mirage of illusory learning they corrupt his mind, and subject it to the temptations of vanity and conceit.

1.2
Vladimir Lenin, *Imperialism, the Highest Stage of Capitalism*, 1916[2]

Vladimir Lenin wrote his pamphlet on imperialism in 1916 in Zurich, when the Great War was raging in Europe. He later admitted that for reasons of censorship, he had to refrain from discussing the revolutionary implications of his analysis. Still, no other

---

2. Source: Daly and Trofimov, eds., *Russia in War and Revolution 1914–1922: A Documentary History* (Indianapolis, IN: Hackett Publishing Company, 2009), 14–16.

text is more critical for understanding his thinking about capitalism, revolution, and the world's future.

Chapter X. The Place of Imperialism in History

We have seen that in its economic essence imperialism is monopoly capitalism. This in itself determines its place in history, for monopoly that grows out of the soil of free competition, and precisely out of free competition, is the transition from the capitalist system to a higher socioeconomic order. We must take special note of the four principal types of monopoly, or principal manifestations of monopoly capitalism, which are characteristic of the epoch we are examining.

Firstly, monopoly arose out of the concentration of production at a very high stage. This refers to the monopolist capitalist associations, cartels, syndicates, and trusts. We have seen the important part these play in present day economic life. At the beginning of the twentieth century, monopolies had acquired complete supremacy in the advanced countries, and although the first steps towards the formation of the cartels were taken by countries enjoying the protection of high tariffs (Germany, America), Great Britain, with her system of free trade, revealed the same basic phenomenon, only a little later, namely, the birth of monopoly out of the concentration of production.

Secondly, monopolies have stimulated the seizure of the most important sources of raw materials, especially for the basic and most highly cartelized industries in capitalist society: the coal and iron industries. The monopoly of the most important sources of raw materials has enormously increased the power of big capital and has sharpened the antagonism between cartelized and non-cartelized industry.

Thirdly, monopoly has sprung from the banks. The banks have developed from modest middleman enterprises into the monopolists of finance capital. Some three to five of the biggest banks in each of the foremost capitalist countries have achieved the "personal link-up" between industrial and bank capital, and have concentrated in their hands the control of thousands upon thousands of millions which form the greater part of the capital and income of entire countries. A financial oligarchy, which throws a close network of dependence relationships over all the economic and political institutions of present-day bourgeois society without exception—such is the most striking manifestation of this monopoly.

Fourthly, monopoly has grown out of colonial policy. To the numerous "old" motives of colonial policy, finance capital has added the struggle for the sources of raw materials, for the export of capital, for spheres of influence, i.e., for spheres for profitable deals, concessions, monopoly profits, and so on, economic territory in general. When the colonies of the European powers, for instance, comprised only one-tenth of the territory of Africa (as was the case in 1876), colonial policy was able to develop—by methods other than those of monopoly—by the "free grabbing" of territories, so to speak. But when nine-tenths of Africa had been seized (by 1900), when the whole world had been divided up, there was inevitably ushered in the era of monopoly possession of colonies and, consequently, of particularly intense struggle for the division and the re-division of the world.

* * *

Monopolies, oligarchy, the striving for domination and not for freedom, the exploitation of an increasing number of small or weak nations by a handful of the richest or most powerful nations—all these have given birth to those distinctive characteristics of imperialism which compel us to define it as parasitic or decaying capitalism.

* * *

The receipt of high monopoly profits by the capitalists in one of the numerous branches of industry, in one of the numerous countries, etc., makes it economically possible for them to bribe certain sections of the workers, and for a time a fairly considerable minority of them, and win them to the side of the bourgeoisie of a given industry or given nation against all the others. The intensification of antagonisms between imperialist nations for the division of the world increases this urge.

1.3
Soldiers Write about the War, 1915–1916[3]

The passages below are taken from soldiers' letters confiscated by military censors. Compiled into summaries for civilian and military officials on the soldiers' "mood," they reveal bitter discontent about conditions at the front, from poor supplies to abusive commanders.

A. Novikov to A. I. Ivanova, Moscow

The elation that the troops felt earlier is no more...

In L'vov, before the eyes of 28 thousand soldiers, five people were flogged for leaving their courtyard without permission to buy white bread.

Anon. to A. P. Nechaeva, Kharkov, July 15, 1915

Cholera is ravaging the entire area. Every day a hundred people are brought from the front; the nearby inhabitants are also sick. The death rate is astronomical.

...I will describe to you the conditions and the treatment of the sick: all of them lie on straw, without mattresses or pillows. There is no disinfection; those who die are buried nearby, behind the huts of the Galicians. There are two doctors and four physicians for 500 sick people. The medical personnel are completely exhausted. Several nurses grew sick from exhaustion and died.

The sick are not isolated; the contagion is spreading...

Efim D. Chernyshev, Belostok, to Aleksandr A. Belikov, Village of Druzh-kovka, Factory of the Toretskii Company, August 3, 1915

We are now so consumed with work day and night that there is no time to look up at the sky, but we are gradually retreating. We have retreated from Lomzha to Belostok. Dear brother, if you could only see what is

---

3. Source: O. Chaadaeva, "Soldatskie pis'ma v gody mirovoi voiny (1915–1917)," *Krasnyi arkhiv* 65–66 (1934): 118–63 (here: 126, 127, 129, 131, 132, 136, 142–43).

going on here! The military transports have stretched over a hundred versts,[4] but most of the people traveling are civilians leaving their homes and going not knowing where, giving themselves up to the mercy of fate. It is a sorry sight to look at: they are driving along cows and pigs, taking whatever they can and leaving the rest for somebody else. You can see children crying, and in some instances parents lose their children, and everywhere you hear the weeping and wailing of the poor Poles, because they are being moved out, and their grain and houses are being burned, so as to leave nothing to the Germans.

Anon. to N. V. Rudakova, Moscow

…But we are still experiencing shortages of shells and rifle bullets. We are all in a bad mood now: it is very unpleasant that the enemy is driving us back. It was fun and good when we were chasing them. We all appreciate that you all, the civilian population, are trying to save Russia and relieve the army, but alas, our superiors are acting in the exact opposite way.

Anon. to S. V. Sukharev, Moscow, November 2, 1916

…There is some news: the Plastun [Cossak] regiment refused to go on the offensive. They are saying: "We are not going without artillery." I don't know what will happen to them. I am writing about it, but if they open the letter, it won't reach you.

Mikh. Vosvizik to Kuz'ma Vosvizik, Village of Kamenets

Tell our relatives and friends to fear military service like fire, because there is neither good footwear, nor clothing, nor food. They don't give us even meat and instead they give us rotten fish and mushrooms with worms. I buy a few things myself, because by sticking to the rations you can die quickly.

Anon. to Novikova, Romanovka, suburb of Odessa

I am alive, thank God, and the devils haven't taken me. Some people are fortunate—they get wounded after two days on the front line. But here it is as if the bullets can't strike you. I am so tired of this dog's life.

---

4. A versta was equal to just over one kilometer or 0.66 miles.

Kh. Grishin to Agaf'ia. Mikh. Grishina, Village of Beguny

…Others think war is just as inevitable as death is inevitable, but I think this is not so, since death is the natural end of existence and creatures, whereas war is an artificial extermination of everything in general and not just of people. I am writing this to you, my dear, so that you will have a correct understanding of war and not think that war is sent by God. War is the result of cunning people's minds and actions, who hold power and, either because they do not know how to use this power properly or for reasons of their own selfish gain, direct matters in such a way that war flares up.

1.4
Order Number One, March 1, 1917[5]

Order Number One was issued by the Petrograd Soviet and pub-lished on March 2, 1917. It prescribed a series of changes in the army's command structure, organization, and even institutional culture. Formally, the order only applied to the Petrograd gar-rison, but it circulated widely and had a shattering effect on the established military order.

To the garrison of the Petrograd District, to all soldiers of the guard, army, artillery, and navy for immediate and precise implementation and to the workers of Petrograd for your information.

The Soviet of Workers' and Soldiers' Deputies decrees:

1. That all companies, battalions, regiments, depots, batteries, squad-rons, ships, and individual branches of military agencies shall imme-diately elect committees of representatives from among the enlisted men of the abovementioned units.

2. That all military units that have not yet elected their representatives to the Soviet of Workers' Deputies shall elect one representative per

---

5. Source: Daly and Trofimov, eds., *Russia in War and Revolution*, 48–50.

company and send them with written credentials to the building of the State Duma on March 2 at 10 a.m.

3. That in all of their political actions military units are subordinate to the Soviet of Workers' and Peasants' Deputies and to their [soldiers'] committees.

4. That the orders of the Military Commission of the State Duma should be complied with, except when they contradict the orders and resolutions of the Soviet of Workers' and Soldiers' Deputies.

5. That weapons of every kind, including rifles, machine guns, armored vehicles, and others, should remain at the disposal and under the control of company and battalion committees [of soldiers], and in no case whatsoever should be given to officers, even at their request.

6. That while on duty and carrying out orders, soldiers must maintain the strictest military discipline, but while off duty and in the capacity of their political, civic, and private life, the civil rights of soldiers cannot in any way be diminished. In particular, that springing to attention and obligatory saluting off duty is abolished.

7. That, moreover, officers shall no longer be addressed as Your Excellency, Your Honor, etc.[6] Instead officers shall be addressed as Mister General, Mister Colonel, etc. The rude treatment of soldiers of any rank and, in particular using the word ty,[7] is forbidden, and any violation of this, as well as all misunderstandings between officers and soldiers should be reported by the latter to the company [soldiers'] committees.

This order should be read in all companies, battalions, regiments, crews, batteries, and other combat and noncombat units.

---

6. Honorific forms of address, such as "Your Honor," were attached to specific ranks, both civil and military, and indicated stature, power, and authority within the governmental structure.

7. In Russian, there are two ways to say "you." One is the respectful "vy," and the other is the familiar "ty." Authority figures in Russia often used the "ty" form as an expression of disrespect and even insult.

1.5
An American in Petrograd, Spring 1917[8]

The following eyewitness account is by Graham Romeyn Taylor (1880–1942), an American sociologist, progressive journalist, and public activist. He traveled in Russia throughout 1917–1918 and worked for the American Committee on Public Information in Vladivostok from late 1918 to March 1919. He conveys the widespread sense of excitement and idealism about the Revolution in spring 1917.

Petrograd, April 3, 1917

Dear father,

I am overwhelmed that I should have been so fortunate as to be here in Russia at this hour of destiny. If you could know even a millionth part of all what I want to tell you and try to make you feel! I can imagine how America hailed the new government. And how proud we all were here that America was the first to recognize it officially. I am filled with great surges of feeling over all it means to the world and the progress of human liberty,—this century advance that has been made in a few days.

* * *

As it was, I landed right in the middle of the great final demonstration— a vast assemblage and parade of troops, all carrying red flags and banners with inscriptions such as "Hail to Free Russia" "Soldiers and Working-men United" "Hurrah for the Constitutional Assembly" and "Liberty, Equality, Fraternity." Every band played the Marseillaise[9] repeatedly, occasionally putting in a popular Russian air....

* * *

---

8. Our thanks to Alex Wilgus for bringing this document to our attention and to the Newberry Library for kind permission to publish this excerpt.
Source: Taylor, Graham Romeyn (son) to Graham Taylor, 1916–1919, 24 1427, Graham Taylor Papers, Newberry Library, Chicago.

9. The French national anthem, written in 1792.

…I never expected to see with my own eyes the Cossacks bearing the red banner of the revolution, and the sudden brotherhood of populace with the men who have so often before at the behest of autocracy ridden them down. The whole thing was a sort of unification of the people—for those Cossacks are of course just like all the rest of the people in the community—they come right from it—and it was surcharged with a wonderful feeling. You knew that it was the great Day of Liberation, of which they had all been dreaming—which they could hardly believe had arrived. It was really a profound spiritual stirring that just got hold of you. It seemed as if the whole great throng was on the point of bursting into tears of happiness. And I confess I felt just that way myself. My mind wandered from the scene to the prisons all over the country, from which at one sweep the political prisoners had been released. I imagined their faces as they came out of the opened doors. I thought of Madam Breshkovskaya[10] out in that village north of Irkutsk and tried to picture the scene when the news of her freedom reached her. I tried to think what would be her emotions if she could see those Cossack troops marching by as they did before her eyes.

It was a day that seemed to lift me to the sky—with a great bright vista spread out—of the future of a people suddenly disclosed to them. I shall never cease my gratitude to heaven that I was permitted to be there. I felt that if there was only some way in which I could put everything I have got into that movement—to take even the smallest part in whatever would help to prevent that lustre from being dimmed—in whatever would make sure that the aspiration is realized in its fullest sense—I would be happier than I could possibly be in doing anything else.

---

10. Ekaterina Breshko-Breshkovskaia (1844–1934) was a veteran revolutionary leader. In February 1917, she was in exile in Minusinsk, eastern Siberia, and was released along with all other political prisoners and exiles.

1.6

Polish Independence and the Russian Revolution, March–April, 1917[11]

On March 16, 1917, in the document excerpted below, the Provisional Government promised Polish independence. This promise, which could not be implemented with Poland under German control, enjoyed widespread Polish support. By the end of the war, the Polish state was reborn, over 120 years after the three successive Partitions of Poland by Russia, Prussia, and Austria in 1772–1795.

Poles! The old state order of Russia, the source of your and our enslavement and disunity, has now been overthrown for good. Liberated Russia, represented by its Provisional Government...hastens to extend its fraternal greetings and invites you to a new life, to freedom.

The old regime made hypocritical promises to you, which it could, but did not wish to, fulfil. The Central Powers took advantage of its mistakes in order to occupy and devastate your territory. With the sole aim of fighting against Russia and her allies, they gave you chimerical state rights...Brother Poles!...Free Russia calls on you to join the ranks of those fighting for peoples' freedom...the Russian people recognize the full right of the fraternal Polish people to determine their own destiny...the Provisional Government considers that the creation of an independent Polish State, comprising all the lands where the Polish people constitute the majority of the population, will be a reliable guarantee for lasting peace in the renewed Europe of the future. United with Russia by a free military alliance, the Polish State will become a firm bulwark of Slavdom against the pressures of the Central Powers...It is up to the Russian Constituent Assembly to give binding strength to the new fraternal alliance and agree to those territorial changes of the Russian State which are necessary for the creation of a free Poland out of all three, currently separated, territories.

---

11. Source: "Vozzvanie Vremennogo Pravitel'stva k poliakam," *Vestnik Vremennogo Pravitel'stva*, no. 11 (57) (March 17/30, 1917), 1.

Accept the fraternal hand, brother Poles, which free Russia extends to you...stand up now to meet the bright new day in your history, the day of the resurrection of Poland...forward, to the struggle, shoulder to shoulder and arm in arm, for your freedom and ours!

1.7

Lenin Calls for a Deepening of the Revolution, April 4, 1917[12]

Vladimir Lenin's "April Theses" speech seemed too radical for most Bolsheviks when he pronounced it. But as the Provisional Government limped from one crisis to another, his call to end the war, depose the Provisional Government, and move towards socialism began to make sense to growing numbers of workers, soldiers, and peasants.

* * *

1) In our attitude towards the war, which under the new government of Lvov[13] and Co. unquestionably remains on Russia's part a predatory imperialist war owing to the capitalist nature of that government, not the slightest concession to "revolutionary defensism" is permissible.

The class-conscious proletariat can give its consent to a revolutionary war, which would really justify revolutionary defensism, only on condition: (a) that power pass to the proletariat and the poorest sections of the peasants aligned with the proletariat; (b) that all annexations be renounced in deed and not in word; (c) that a complete break be effected in actual fact with all capitalist interests.

* * *

---

12. Source: Daly and Trofimov, eds., *Russia in War and Revolution*, 71–73.

13. Prince Georgii Lvov (1861–1925) was the first prime minister in the Provisional Government.

2) The specific feature of the present situation in Russia is that the country is *passing* from the first stage of the revolution—which, owing to the insufficient class-consciousness and organization of the proletariat, placed power in the hands of the bourgeoisie—to its second stage, which must place power in the hands of the proletariat and the poorest sections of the peasants.

This transition is characterized, on the one hand, by a maximum of legally recognized rights (Russia is *now* the freest of all the belligerent countries in the world); on the other, by the absence of violence towards the masses, and, finally, by their unreasoning trust in the government of capitalists, those worst enemies of peace and socialism....

3) No support for the Provisional Government; the utter falsity of all its promises should be made clear, particularly of those relating to the renunciation of annexations....

4) Recognition of the fact that in most of the Soviets of Workers' Deputies our [Bolshevik] Party is in a minority, so far a small minority, as against a bloc of all the petty-bourgeois opportunist elements, from the Popular Socialists and the Socialist-Revolutionaries down to the [Menshevik] Organizing Committee...who have yielded to the influence of the bourgeoisie and spread that influence among the proletariat.

The masses must be made to see that the Soviets of Workers' Deputies are the only possible form of revolutionary government, and that therefore our task is, as long as this government yields to the influence of the bourgeoisie, to present a patient, systematic, and persistent explanation of the errors of their tactics, an explanation especially adapted to the practical needs of the masses....

5) Not a parliamentary republic—to return to a parliamentary republic from the Soviets of Workers' Deputies would be a retrograde step—but a republic of Soviets of Workers', Agricultural Laborers' and Peasants' Deputies throughout the country, from top to bottom.

Abolition of the police, the army and the bureaucracy.[14]

The salaries of all officials, all of whom are elective and displaceable at any time, not to exceed the average wage of a competent worker.

6) The weight of emphasis in the agrarian program to be shifted to the Soviets of Agricultural Laborers' Deputies. Confiscation of all landed estates.

---

14. I.e., the standing army to be replaced by the arming of the whole people. (Footnote added by Lenin.)

Nationalization of *all* lands in the country, the land to be disposed of by the local Soviets of Agricultural Laborers' and Peasants' Deputies....

7) The *immediate* union of all banks in the country into a single national bank and the institution of control over it by the Soviet of Workers' Deputies.

8) It is not our immediate task "to introduce" socialism, but only to bring social production and the distribution of products at once under the control of the Soviets of Workers' Deputies....

10) A renewed International....

1.8
General Session of the Petrograd Soviet, September 11, 1917[15]

At the September 11 session of the Petrograd Soviet, Leon Trotsky stepped up to confront the Menshevik leader Fedor Dan (1871–1947) and to offer a more radical program of action, as documented below. Two weeks later, the Bolsheviks were in control of the Petrograd Soviet's Executive Committee, with Trotsky at the helm.

Fedor Dan: Russia is currently experiencing days more difficult than at any point during our revolution. Our revolution emerged in the midst of such hardships that were never experienced by any other revolution. A three-year war and the resultant economic collapse make it difficult for the revolution not only to develop but to preserve the gains it has made so far.

Moreover, one should not overlook the fact that the army played an extraordinary role in our revolution and that the proletariat, given the nature of our economic development, cannot play the role it does in Western Europe. This is why from the very beginning we realized that the continuing collapse [*razrukha*] would pose enormous difficulties for

---

15. Source: "V Petrogr. Sovete rabochikh i soldatsk. deputatov," *Izvestiia*, no. 169 (September 13, 1917): 4.

us and that every revolutionary should focus on the political indoctrination of the worker and soldier masses....

They are saying that all power should be in the hands of the soldiers, workers, and peasants. But if you read the Bolsheviks' resolutions and publications, you will see something entirely different: power is offered to the proletariat and not to the peasantry as a whole, but only to its poorest members, i.e. agricultural laborers. But you should not forget that the vast majority of peasants does not share the viewpoint of the proletariat. Indeed, were the proletariat of Petrograd to write off the peasantry from the revolution, I assert, that will be the end of our revolution, which would be drowned in blood, since, under those circumstances, we would receive not a single train-car load of grain from the villages, and a hunger-driven uprising of the angry masses would finish off our revolution once and for all.

* * *

I think that all of the programs that would unite only revolutionaries are not worth a kopek. If we really want to overcome all of the challenges, we must draft a program that will appeal to dozens of millions of peasants and all of the urban dwellers. We heard here that we should offer peace to all nations, but we have repeatedly stated this since March 14. [Shouts from the audience: "Not true!"]. I don't know what the comrade who yelled this has done for peace, but one should look at what the Soviet has been doing throughout. [Shouting from the audience: "but the government did not appeal to other governments with an offer of peace!"]....

* * *

Leon Trotsky: Comrade Dan tells us that the Russian revolution has faced greater difficulties than any revolution in history. But the more difficulties we face, the more radical should the means be for surmounting them. Yet after seven months, we still do not even have a Constituent Assembly, something that has never happened in any other revolution.[16] ...

---

16. The American equivalent, the Constitutional Convention, met in 1787, ten years after the start of the Revolution.

Dan is referring to Western Europe, but nothing like the political situation that the Russian Republic is now experiencing ever occurred there. There are two ways—one is to use capital punishment and other repressive measures to create a combat ready army and strangle the revolution and the other is to give the broad masses what they want.

* * *

You now stand in the middle and you are offered two hands—one is the hand of the bourgeoisie, the other is the hand of the proletariat of Petrograd and Moscow....

Resolution of the Soviet: The programmatic section of the resolution was adopted by a huge majority of the assembled. It included the following; 1) prompt and merciless liquidation of the Kornilov conspiracy;[17] 2) abolition of the death penalty; 3) focusing all efforts on the speediest achievement of a general peace on the basis of the demands of the Russian revolution; 4) convocation of a Constituent Assembly on schedule; 5) immediate dissolution of the State Duma and the State Council; 6) transfer of all land to the jurisdiction of land committees, temporarily until the Constituent Assembly; 7) on the workers' issue, introduction of state control over production through worker organizations, implementation of an 8-hour work day; decisive struggle against viciously deliberate closings of enterprises, against excessive profits of the capitalists and against mass unemployment. In the army: a radical purging of the commanding ranks from top to bottom to get rid of all individuals who have not embraced the spirit of the new democratic army and are not willing to work jointly with the soldier organizations.

---

17. As commander-in-chief, Lavr Kornilov (1870–1918) thought he had the approval of Prime Minister Kerensky to restore order in Petrograd in late August, but the effort was thwarted.

1.9
Declaration of the Rights of the Working and Exploited People, January 1918[18]

Vladimir Lenin intended this Declaration to evoke the Declara-
tion of the Rights of Man and Citizen passed by the French revo-
lutionaries in August 1789. The Bolshevik Revolution, in his view,
would go beyond the French Revolution, transforming the world
not only politically but also economically. The Declaration was
voted down by the democratically elected Constituent Assembly.
The Bolsheviks used the Assembly's failure to adopt the Declara-
tion as a pretext to dissolve the Assembly the following day. But
its main intended audience was neither the Constituent Assembly
nor the Third Congress of Soviets, which approved it on January
18, but the working people of the world.

The Constituent Assembly resolves:

I.   1. Russia is hereby proclaimed a Republic of Soviets of Workers', Soldiers', and Peasants' Deputies. All power, centrally and locally, is vested in these Soviets.

2. The Russian Soviet Republic is established on the principle of a free union of free nations, as a federation of Soviet national republics.

II. Its fundamental aim being to abolish all exploitation of man by man, to completely eliminate the division of society into classes, to mercilessly crush the resistance of the exploiters, to establish a socialist organization of society, and to achieve the victory of socialism in all countries, the Constituent Assembly further resolves:

1. Private ownership of land is hereby abolished. All land together with all buildings, farm implements, and other appurtenances of agricultural production, is proclaimed the property of the entire working people.

2. The Soviet laws on workers' control and on the Supreme Economic Council are hereby confirmed for the purpose of guaranteeing the

---

18. Source: Daly and Trofimov, eds., *Russia in War and Revolution*, 145–47.

power of the working people over the exploiters and as a first step towards the complete conversion of the factories, mines, railways, and other means of production and transport into the property of the workers' and peasants' state.

3. The conversion of all banks into the property of the workers' and peasants' state is hereby confirmed as one of the conditions for the emancipation of the working people from the yoke of capital.

4. For the purpose of abolishing the parasitic sections of society, universal labor conscription is hereby instituted.

5. To ensure the sovereign power of the working people, and to eliminate all possibility of the restoration of the power of the exploiters, the arming of the working people, the creation of a socialist Red Army of workers and peasants, and the complete disarming of the propertied classes are hereby decreed.

III. 1. Expressing its firm determination to wrest mankind from the clutches of finance capital and imperialism, which have in this most criminal of wars drenched the world in blood, the Constituent Assembly wholeheartedly endorses the policy pursued by Soviet power of denouncing secret treaties, organizing the most extensive fraternization with the workers and peasants of the armies in the war, and achieving at all costs, by revolutionary means, a democratic peace between the nations, without annexations and indemnities and on the basis of the free self-determination of nations.

2. With the same end in view, the Constituent Assembly insists on a complete break with the barbarous policy of bourgeois civilization, which has built the prosperity of the exploiters belonging to a few chosen nations on the enslavement of hundreds of millions of working people in Asia, in the colonies in general, and in the small countries. The Constituent Assembly welcomes the policy of the Council of People's Commissars in proclaiming the complete independence of Finland, commencing the evacuation of troops from Persia, and proclaiming freedom of self-determination for Armenia.

3. The Constituent Assembly regards the Soviet law on the cancellation of the loans contracted by the governments of the tsar, the landowners, and the bourgeoisie as a first blow struck at international banking, finance capital, and expresses the conviction that Soviet

power will firmly pursue this path until the international workers'
uprising against the yoke of capital has completely triumphed.

* * *

1.10
Mustafa Chokaev, Reminiscences of 1917–1918[19]

A Muslim Kazakh political activist, Mustafa Chokaev (1890–
1941), served as prime minister in the Provisional Government of
Autonomous Turkestan from November 1917 to February 1918.
He asserts that he had envisioned Turkestan as an autonomous
part of a democratic Russian state, but the Bolshevik dissolution
of the Constitutional Assembly left him no choice but to fight for
an independent Turkestan.

We did not discuss Turkestan's autonomy at our congresses. But in the
depths of our national and regional committees it was the most frequent
topic of our conversations. We viewed autonomy this way: Turkestan
should have its own legislative body and an autonomous government.
The central all-Russian "federal" authority should be in charge of foreign policy, state finance, railroads, and the military. The local autonomous government should exercise control over schools, local railroad
construction, town and provincial institutions of self-government, the
land issue—we particularly emphasized this, and the judiciary. We also
wanted to introduce some substantial reforms into the area of the formation of the army, namely, we envisioned the creation of a "territorial
army," i.e., for Turkestanis to perform military service in Turkestan, while
remaining under a unified all-Russian command. That was, of course,
only principles, only a sketch. We did not go farther into the details. Our
main concern was the question of Turkestani personnel. One can proclaim any principles, wish for anything at all, even for the moon in the

---

19. Source: Daly and Trofimov, eds., *Russia in War and Revolution*, 282–84.

sky. Yet if adequate personnel are lacking, if there are no technical experts, no human resources, then all of these beautiful wishes will remain empty words, capable only of provoking the derision of enemies and misleading friends and the popular masses, on whose behalf and for whose good these principles are proposed and these beautiful slogans are proclaimed. I will not say that we did not have any such human resources, but they were extremely insufficient....

I would like briefly to recount the last episode of our struggle. Kokand was already under fire. Machine guns and rifles were crackling. Hand grenades were exploding. Once in a while cannons boomed! The Bolsheviks sent us their first "parliamentarians" with the proposal to hand me over to the Kokand military revolutionary committee.[20] I received them in the presence of all the available members of the government. Without waiting for the opinion of my comrades, I responded that I was ready to surrender myself to the military revolutionary committee on the condition that the Bolsheviks immediately cease shelling the city and pledge not to apply repressive measures toward civilians. The Bolshevik parliamentarians left and returned only two days later. By that time Kokand was besieged from all sides. Bolshevik troops were arriving from Samarkand, Tashkent, and Fergana. Our people were also arriving, but they were armed with long iron-tipped pikes, sickles, axes, pitchforks, big knives, and, in the best cases, hunting rifles. Their most potent weapon was their hatred of the Bolsheviks. None could doubt the outcome of this struggle. I remember as if it were yesterday how at 11:20 a.m. new Bolshevik parliamentarians arrived with a new ultimatum. Now the Bolsheviks demanded: (1) the autonomous government's recognition of the Soviet government; (2) its issuing of an appeal to the population of Turkestan to obey the Soviet government; (3) disarming the population and handing over all of its weapons to the Bolsheviks; (4) disbanding the militia. And so forth. There were four members of the government present....Our response was brief: we refused to accept the ultimatum. On behalf of my comrades I told the Bolshevik parliamentarians: "Strength is on your side. Except for our conviction that justice is on our side, we have none. We do not doubt that you will defeat us, but recognizing your right to rule, recognizing the Soviet government of Turkestan is something we cannot do!"

---

20. From late October 1917 to March 1918, the Bolsheviks set up over 220 local military revolutionary committees endowed with almost complete autonomy and authority to coordinate the seizure of power.

1.11
Aleksandra Kollontai, "Soon!"
(in 48 Years' Time), 1919[21]

Aleksandra Kollontai (1872–1952) wholeheartedly embraced the Russian Revolution. Appointed People's Commissar for Social Welfare in Lenin's government in October 1917, she was the first woman in the world to hold a ministerial position. In the early 1920s she led Zhenotdel, the Women's Section of the Bolshevik Party's Central Committee. Following her disagreement with Lenin over the role of trade unions in the Soviet system, she was appointed Soviet Ambassador to Norway, another unprecedented appointment. Her visionary essay, excerpted below from a 1922 reprint, describes a communist future with no class conflict or violence.

January 7, 1970. The "House of Rest," is filled with light, warmth, and commotion. It is the final residence of old veterans of "the Great Years" of the World Revolution. On this day, which used to be Christmas, the veterans decided to recall the days of their childhood and youth and to decorate a Christmas tree, a real Christmas tree, like the ones before the global transformation. The young adults, teenagers, and children were enthusiastic, especially when they learned that "the red grandmother" would be reminiscing about the great year of 1917.

* * *

But a closer look at the youth revealed that this was no longer the youth that had fought at the barricades during "the Great Years," and even less so the youth that had lived under the yoke of capitalism.

* * *

There was not a single sick, pale, or exhausted face among the youth of the commune who gathered for the Christmas party. Their inquisitive

---

21. Source: A. Kolontai (*sic*), *Skoro* (*cherez 48 let*), Miniatiurnaia Biblioteka, no. 1 (Omsk: Izdatel'stvo Sibbiuro TsKRKSM, 1922), 3, 4, 6–7, 8, 11, 12.

eyes were glowing with fervor; their firm, elastic youthful bodies moved boldly, supplely, and rhythmically. But most joyful of all was that incessant peels of merry laughter filled the bright celebration hall.

The youth of "Commune No. 10" loved life, loved laughter, and frowned only when it had to confront the only remaining enemy of mankind—nature.

* * *

But the youth loved this struggle. What would life be like without struggle, without the surmounting of challenges, without the mind's audacious aspirations, without the eternal drive forward—into the unknown, toward the unreachable!

Without this struggle life in the commune would have become boring....Life [in the commune] is organized in such a way that people live not in families, but are divided up according to age. Children live in "Palaces of the Child," young men and women in jolly little houses surrounded by gardens, and adults live in dormitories of various types, such as the "Home of Rest" for old people.

There are neither rich nor poor in the communes. These are forgotten words. They no longer mean anything. Commune members have everything necessary, so as not to have to worry about their daily and material needs. Clothing, food, books, entertainment—the commune delivers everything. In return, commune members lend the commune their working hands for two hours per day and their creativity, the audacious pursuits of their minds for the rest of their lives.

The commune has no enemies, since all the neighboring peoples and nations have long since established similar communes and the entire world is now a federation of communes. The younger generation no longer knows what war is…

* * *

"And I [know] what a ruble is and what money in general is. We saw money in a museum. Grandpa, did you also have money? And did you carry it in a sack in your pocket? And were there—what did they call them?—pickpockets who snatched it, right? That's really funny."

And ringing voices joined together in friendly laughter, while the veterans of the revolution felt rather embarrassed for that distant past when there were capitalists, thieves, money, aristocratic ladies ...

* * *

"And you, 'Red Grandmother,' did you shoot at a human being? A live human being?"

The eyes of the commune youths gazed with astonishment and flashed a reproach, bewilderment ... To shoot at a live human being? ... But life is sacred! ...

"But we ourselves were prepared to die! We sacrificed everything for the revolution," "Red Grandmother" offered by way of explanation.

"Like us for our commune," proudly reply the young people.

...

You made it, so will we. You subjugated social forces. We will subjugate nature.... Your Christmas tree celebration is in the past. Ours lies ahead! Life is not an accomplishment; it is the struggle itself, a never-ending rebellious pursuit!

1.12
Nikolai Bukharin and Evgenii
Preobrazhenskii, *ABC of Communism*[22]

In early 1919, Nikolai Bukharin and Evgenii Preobrazhenskii (1886–1937) published the ABC of Communism *in order to summarize Bolshevik beliefs. Bukharin was the editor of the Bolshevik flagship newspaper* Pravda *and a leading member of the Communist Party. He had opposed the Treaty of Brest-Litovsk in favor of launching a struggle for "world revolution." He is the*

---

22. Source: N. Bukharin and E. Preobrazhensky, *The ABC of Communism: A Popular Explanation of the Program of the Communist Party of Russia*, trans. Eden and Cedar Paul (London: The Communist Party of Great Britain, 1922), 262–63, 266–67, 284, 285–87, 333–34.

author of the excerpts from Chapter 12. Preobrazhenskii was a member of Pravda's editorial board and is the author of the excerpt from Chapter 15. Both were killed during the Stalinist Terror in the later 1930s.

CHAPTER TWELVE
THE ORGANIZATION OF INDUSTRY

* * *

§ 94.

Our Goal, the Development of Productivity. The foundation of our whole policy must be the widest possible development of productivity. The disorganization of production has been so extensive, the post-war scarcity of all products is so conspicuous, that everything else must be subordinated to this one task. More products! More boots, scythes, barrels, textiles, salt, clothing, corn, etc.—these are our primary need. How can the desired end be secured? Only by increasing the productive forces of the country, by increased productivity. There is no other way. But here we encounter a formidable difficulty, arising out of the onslaught made upon us by the worldwide forces of the counter-revolution. We are blockaded and put upon our defense, so that we are simultaneously deprived of labor power and cut off from the material means of production. We have to wrest by force of arms petroleum and coal from the landlords and capitalists. Here is our first great task. We have to set the work of production upon a proper footing. Here is our second great task.

* * *

NEVERTHELESS, ONE OF THE FUNDAMENTAL TASKS OF THE SOVIET POWER WAS AND IS THAT OF UNITING ALL THE ECONOMIC ACTIVITIES OF THE COUNTRY IN ACCORDANCE WITH A GENERAL PLAN OF DIRECTION

BY THE STATE. Thus only is it possible to retain productivity at such a level as will permit a subsequent farther development. We have learned in Part One that one of the great merits of the communist system is that it puts an end to the chaos, to the "anarchy," of the capitalist system. Herein lies the very essence of communism.

§ 100.

Comradely Labor Discipline.

* * *

Labor discipline must be based upon the feeling and *the consciousness that every worker is responsible to his class,* upon the consciousness that slackness and carelessness are treason to the common cause of the workers. The capitalists no longer exist as a dominant caste. The workers no longer work for capitalists, usurers, and bankers; they work for themselves....

* * *

It is plain that the work of creating a new labor discipline will be arduous, for it will involve *the re-education of the masses.* A slave psychology and slavish habits are still deeply ingrained. It is just as it was in the case of the army.... The re-education of the workers will be facilitated by the fact that the toiling masses themselves realize (and have been taught by daily experience) that their fate is in their own hands. They had a very good lesson when for a time, in various regions, the Soviet Power was overthrown by the counter-revolution. For instance, in the Urals, in Siberia, etc.

The communists, the workers' vanguard, gave a striking example of the new, comradely discipline when they instituted the so-called *Communist Saturdays,* when they worked voluntarily and gratuitously, increasing the productivity of labor far beyond the ordinary.

* * *

CHAPTER FIFTEEN
THE ORGANIZATION OF BANKS AND MONETARY CIRCULATION

* * *

§121.

Money and the Dying-out of the Monetary System. Communist society will know nothing of money. Every worker will produce goods for the general welfare. He will not receive any certificate to the effect that he has delivered the product to society; he will receive no money, that is to say. In like manner, he will pay no money to society when he receives whatever he requires from the common store. A very different state of affairs prevails in socialist society, which is inevitable as an intermediate stage between capitalism and communism. Here money is needed, for it has a part to play in commodity economy. If I, as a boot maker, need a coat, I change my wares, the boots that I make, into money. Money is a commodity by means of which I can procure any other commodity I may please, and by means of which in the given case I can procure the particular thing I want, namely a coat. Every producer of commodities acts in the same way. In socialist society, this commodity economy will to some extent persist.

Socialism, however, is communism in course of construction; it is incomplete communism. In proportion as the work of upbuilding communism is successfully effected, the need for money will disappear. In due time the State will probably be compelled to put an end to the expiring monetary circulation. This will be of especial importance in order to bring about the final disappearance of the laggards of the bourgeois classes who with hoarded money will continue to consume values created by the workers in a society which has proclaimed: "He who does not work, neither shall he eat."

* * *

1.13
The Fate of Kiev, 1918[23]

With the collapse of Imperial Russia, Ukraine became the object of competing powers and interests. The autonomous Ukrainian government was overthrown by pro-Bolshevik forces in February 1918. In March, German troops drove out the Bolsheviks. On April 29, with German acquiescence, the Cossack General Pavlo Skoropadskii (1873–1945) seized power in Kiev.

　　The author of the memoir excerpted below, Nikolai Mogilianskii (1871–1934), was an ethnographer and a member of the liberal Kadet Party. Like many Russian liberals, he supported the cultural autonomy of Ukraine but opposed its independence. More instability and violence followed the events recorded by Mogilianskii.

...on January 17 (30) as the brief, foggy winter day was drawing to a close, we were approaching Kiev, and the train had to stop every minute since Kiev Station Number One was not accessible. With every stop, infrequent shelling was heard....

　　These were the first salvos fired at Kiev by the Bolshevik army under the command of Remnev. The first act of the Kiev tragedy in the long-suffering year 1918 began. Since Kiev's capture by Batu [Khan] in the thirteenth century,[24] the city has not seen anything like this.

* * *

Kiev was left to the mercy of fate by the fleeing Ukrainian troops and authorities. The Bolshevik troops, who stormed into the city on January 26 and at that moment looked more like a gang, and their nightmarish "activities" soon made people forget the nightmare and horror of the [preceding] nine-day artillery bombardment. The greenish faces of the city

---

23. Source: N. M. Mogilianskii, "Tragediia Ukrainy" in *Arkhiv russkoi revoliutsii*, 22 vols., ed. I. V. Gessen (Berlin: Slowo-Verlag, 1922–1937; Moscow: Terra, 1993): 11:77, 79, 80, 83.

24. Batu Khan (c. 1207–1255) was a Mongol ruler whose forces conquered nearly all of the Rus' principalities in 1237–1240 with great violence.

dwellers, exhausted by hunger, lack of sleep, and recent worries were now distorted by the horror of madness and a dull, exhausted hopelessness.

What followed was a stomach-turning massacre in the most direct sense of the word, the totally indiscriminate and arbitrary killing of those Russian officers who had remained in the city and did not want to join Ukrainians in their fight against the Bolsheviks. From hotels and private apartments, unfortunate officers were dragged literally like cattle to slaughter to the "Dukhonin Headquarters"[25]—the ironic name of the Mariinskii park—a favorite execution spot where hundreds of officers of the Russian army perished. For example, my cousin Colonel A. M. Rechitskii was murdered on Bibikov Boulevard with a shot to the back of his head when he resisted four Red Army men who had wanted to tear off his epaulettes....[26]

* * *

Besides officers, anyone who was naïve enough to display their red card, that is, their Ukrainian citizenship certificate, was also executed....

* * *

Soon, however, vague rumors surfaced that the Ukrainians had struck a deal with the Germans and that German troops were moving on Kiev. These rumors were validated by the Bolsheviks' behavior. Sensing that the ground under their feet was shaking, they behaved like lords for a day: plundering, feasting, destroying, and rejoicing, seizing the moment, however brief!

The conditions of city dwellers deteriorated by the day. Gangs of armed bandits emerged, robbing people at night, attacking residents and their dwellings. Having been disarmed by the Bolsheviks, poor city dwellers lacked even the most basic means of self-defense.

---

25. Nikolai Dukhonin (1876–1917), the last commander-in-chief of the Imperial Russian Army, was murdered by a mob of pro-Bolshevik sailors on December 2, 1917 (O.S.). To send someone "to Dukhonin's headquarters" was a euphemism that meant to kill him.

26. Military epaulettes were considered by ordinary Russians to be an egregious symbol of the old repressive order.

Only after the Bolsheviks had loaded up all kinds of valuables and had fled from the city, two or three days before the German attack, did the organization of self-defense begin.

* * *

Having signed on to all the German conditions in Brest,[27] the Ukrainians entered Kiev as triumphant victors. Discreetly, however, the Germans had entered the city the day before in order to ensure the establishment of order. This was on February 17 (O.S).[28]

* * *

Once the Germans arrived, all robberies and violence ceased as if by waving a magic wand, without any threats or menacing declarations. City dwellers breathed easier. Even late at night it became completely safe to walk the streets. Theaters, cinemas, and restaurants reopened and life began to play its eternally hectic music in double time.

Ukrainian patriots afforded themselves the luxury of only a few extreme savageries so that, as I was informed, only one Jewish student was its casualty, killed in the Podol[29] for an unknown reason and under entirely unclear circumstances. In any case, there were none of the horrible murders and assassinations that had marked the period of Bolshevik rule....

* * *

Anarchy was held at bay by only one force—German arms. So how did the Germans comport themselves in the Ukrainian countryside? Everything depended, of course, on the character of the commander. I personally observed Germans keeping guard in villages of Kanevskii district in Kiev province. They did not irritate the population and did not leave any bad feelings. They paid for all the foodstuffs they took from the people and did not insult them.

---

27. That is, having signed a separate treaty in Brest-Litovsk with the Central Powers on February 9, 1918.

28. That is, March 2 (N.S.).

29. The Podil (in Ukrainian) was an old commercial quarter of the city.

In other places, however—and I read a number of detailed reports and investigative protocols about this—direct, shameless and cynical plunder occurred....

1.14
The Russian "Internationale," 1902–1944

The "Internationale," a song composed in France in 1871 after the crushing of the socialist Paris Commune, soon became a rallying hymn of the international socialist movement. Its Russian translation appeared in 1902. In 1918, the Bolsheviks adopted the song's first three stanzas below as Soviet Russia's state anthem. By doing so, they sought to position themselves as the rightful champions and heirs of the century-old fight on behalf of the oppressed masses. Even after it was replaced by a new Stalinist state anthem in 1944, the Russian "Internationale" remained the official song of the Soviet and now Russian Communist Party.

Rise up, ye branded with a curse,
World of the hungry and enslaved!
Our minds are boiling with anger.
We are ready for mortal combat.
The whole world of violence we will
Shatter to the ground, and then
Our own, new world we will build;
He who was nobody will become all.

Chorus:
This is our last
And decisive battle;
With the strains of the Internationale
The human race will rise up! × 2

No one will grant us deliverance:
Neither god, nor king, nor hero.

We will achieve liberation
By our own hand.
To overthrow oppression with a skillful hand,
To fight for our rightful due,
Blow the horn and boldly forge,
Strike while the iron is hot!

Chorus × 2
Only we, toilers of the great,
Global army of labor,
Are entitled to possess the earth,
Not the parasites—they never!
And if mighty thunder blasts
The pack of dogs and executioners,
The sun will keep shining its
Bright rays on us all.

Chorus × 2

1.15
Appeal of Rebel Leaders to the Peasant Masses, Late July/Early August 1920[30]

Aleksander Sapozhkov was a division commander fighting for the Bolsheviks on the Eastern and the Southern Fronts. Angry about his sudden dismissal in July 1920, he mutinied, and his 9th Cavalry Division followed him. What started as a personal grudge quickly developed into a popular rebellion, as growing numbers of peasants of Samara province (in the Middle Volga region) joined the rebellion. The Bolsheviks responded with full

---

30. Source: Tsentr dokumentatsii noveishei istorii Saratovskoi oblasti, f. 27, op. 1, d. 534, l. 14.

military force. By early September, the rebels had been defeated and dispersed, but even larger peasant rebellions followed.

Our dear comrades, fathers and brothers...

Today the 1st Red Army of "Truth" has come to your area. What are these troops and what is the goal of their arrival you probably do not know. We will try to explain it to you briefly, so that you can see in us your defenders, your children and sons who have come to help you and to liberate you at last from the horror and violence, to which you have been subjected for more than a year.

Our army fought on the Ural Front where it performed many heroic deeds and underwent many trials and deprivations in order to defend you from the external enemy. While on the frontlines, we received thousands of letters from our fathers and brothers who lived here, in the rear. All of them were filled with moans and complaints about the violent abuses, scandals, humiliations, deprivations of property and even of life that were being carried out on behalf of the people, on behalf of the People's Soviet Power, that is, supposedly on your own behalf. It all happened because under the guise of the love of freedom, dishonest people began to infiltrate our honest family of laborers. These people did not understand the real life of the laboring peasants and the working class. They were former bourgeois, landlords, generals, village policemen, and other such scum, which like leeches pierced the body of the Russian people and began to drink its blood without any mercy. Why did this happen, how could we not prevent this and instead allowed all kinds of scoundrels to enslave us? This happened because the ruling party of communists seized power in the country and began to implement a dictatorship, which is the absolute power of just one party of communists, not a dictatorship of the proletariat as it was really supposed to be.

Members of the party of communists were put in all places regardless of whether they were honest or thieves, friends of the people or disguised parasites who had joined the party only in order to live at the expense of poor peasants. So come to us, assist us, and we will rescue you from all the evils and troubles that weigh you down. We are the same working and laboring people as you are. We are your children and sons. It pains us to hear your moans. It pains us to see your endless suffering, and we have come to rescue you from all that. The cities and villages we have taken prove to us that we are not mistaken, and that you support and understand, since you have experienced all this in your own lives.

* * *

Long live the Army of "Truth"! Long live victory over our enemies! Long live the true fighters for the revolution of the working people!

Section 2
The Bolsheviks Engage the World

2.1
The Bolsheviks Take Russia Out of World War I, January–March 1918[31]

*The first major security crisis to face Soviet Russia was the loom-
ing prospect of its defeat in the Great War. The excerpts below
shed light on the negotiations at Brest-Litovsk. The head of the
Soviet delegation, Leon Trotsky, explains why the Bolsheviks
refused to agree to the harsh German demands, and General
Max von Hoffmann, the chief of staff of the German armies on
the Eastern Front, shares his recollections of the talks. Instead of
the German workers rising up, as anticipated by the Bolsheviks,
a major German offensive ensued, compelling the Bolsheviks to
agree to even harsher terms several weeks later.*

Leon Trotsky, "At Brest-Litovsk," May 1918

* * *

At the same time, we pointed out that we were going to Brest-Litovsk for
the continuance of the peace negotiations under conditions which were
becoming better for ourselves but worse for our enemies. We observed

---

31. Sources: N. Lenin and Leon Trotsky, *The Proletarian Revolution in Russia*, ed. Louis
C. Fraina (New York: The Communist Press, 1918), 350–52, 353; Max von Hoffmann,
The War of Lost Opportunities (London: K. Paul, French, Trubner & Co., Ltd., 1924),
216, 219–20, 226, 227–28.

the movement in Austria-Hungary[32] and there was much to indicate—
for that is what the Social Democratic deputies in the Reichstag had
reference to—that Germany too was on the eve of such events. Filled
with this hope, we departed.[33] And even during the first days of our
next stay at Brest, a radiogram via Vilna brought us the first news that
in Berlin a tremendous strike movement had broken out,[34] which, just
as that of Austria-Hungary, was directly connected with the conduct of
the negotiations at Brest-Litovsk. But, as is often the case in accordance
with the dialectics of the class struggle, the very dimensions of this proletarian movement—never seen in Germany before—compelled a closing
of the ranks of the propertied classes and forced them to ever greater
implacability....

* * *

...Then came the hour of decision. We could not declare war. We were
too weak. The army had lost internal cohesion. For the salvation of our
country and in order to overcome the process of disintegration, we were
forced to re-establish the inner connection of the working-masses. This
psychological bond can be created by way of common productive effort
in the fields, in the factories, and in the workshops. We must bring the
working masses, so long subjected to the terrible sufferings and catastrophic trials of the war, back to their fields and factories where they can
again find themselves in their labour and enable us to build up internal
discipline. This is the only way out for a country that must now do pen-
ance for the sins of Czarism and of the bourgeoisie. We are forced to
give up this war and to lead the army out of this slaughter. But we do
declare at the same *time* and in the face of German militarism: the peace
you have forced upon us is a peace of force and robbery. We shall not
permit that you, diplomatic gentlemen, can say to the German workers:

---

32. Trotsky was referring to the food crisis that gripped Austria-Hungary in winter
1917–1918, precipitating widespread unrest, including a strike movement in the main
industrial centers.

33. Trotsky had arrived for his first round of negotiations on January 6 (N.S.) and, following a twelve-day recess, returned just before the 28th.

34. Major strikes encompassing up to one million workers commenced on January 28
in several German cities. Among the strikers' demands was an end to the war on Soviet
Russian terms.

"You have called our demands conquests and annexations, but see: we bring to you, under these same demands, the signature of the Russian Revolution!"—Yes, we are weak; we can not now conduct a war, but we possess sufficient revolutionary force to prove that we shall not, voluntarily, place our signatures under a treaty that you write with your sword upon the bodies of living people. We refused our signatures!—I believe, comrades, that we acted rightly.

* * *

Max von Hoffmann, *The War of Lost Opportunities*

* * *

Trotsky was certainly the most interesting personality in the new Russian Government: clever, versatile, cultured, possessing great energy, power of work, and eloquence, he gave the impression of a man who knew exactly what he wanted and who would not be deterred from using any means for the attainment of his end. The question has been much discussed whether he came with the intention of concluding a peace, or if from the very beginning he only wanted to find the most visible platform from which to propagandize his Bolshevik theories. Although propaganda played such a prominent part in the whole of the negotiations of the following weeks, I still think that Trotsky at first wanted to try to make peace and that it was only afterwards, when he had been driven into a corner by Kuhlmann's[35] dialectics, for which he was no match, that he thought of bringing the conference to a spectacular finish by declaring that, though Russia could not accept the conditions of peace offered by the Central Powers, nor even fully discuss them, still, it declared the War to be finished.

* * *

When I finished there was profound silence. Even Mr. Trotsky, at the first moment, could not find a word in reply. It was difficult to find anything

---

35. Richard von Kühlmann (1873–1948) was Germany's foreign minister.

to say against it, as all I had asserted was in strict accordance with facts. The meeting was quickly adjourned.

* * *

...In the meeting of the 10th of February he announced, that although he would sign no Treaty of Peace, Russia would consider the War at an end from that time, she would send all her Armies to their homes and that she would proclaim the fact to all the Peoples and all the States.

The whole congress sat speechless when Trotsky had finished his declaration. We were all dumbfounded....If peace were not concluded the object of the armistice was not attained, and, therefore, the armistice came automatically to an end, and hostilities must recommence. Trotsky's declaration was, in my opinion, nothing more than a denouncement of the Armistice.

* * *

On the eighth day after the negotiations had been broken off so abruptly by Trotsky, the Eastern Army resumed the offensive. The demoralized Russian troops offered no kind of resistance, if it were possible even to call them troops, as it was only the staffs that still remained; the bulk of the troops had already gone home. We simply swept over the whole of Livonia and Estonia, and took possession of them. Our troops were greeted everywhere as deliverers from the Bolshevik terror, and not only by the Baltic Germans, but likewise by the Letts and Estonians.

Two days after our advance had recommenced a wireless message was received from Petrograd announcing that the Russians were ready to renew the negotiations and conclude a Peace and also begging that the German advance might be stopped. It had very quickly been proved that Trotsky's theories could not resist facts. The German Army advanced only as far as Lake Peipus and Narva,[36] in order to release at least all the Baltic members of our race from the Bolsheviks and all their crimes. Then the advance was stopped and the Bolsheviks were informed that they might send a delegation, authorized to sign a Peace, to Brest-Litovsk.

---

36. An Estonian city 150 km from St. Petersburg.

Almost immediately the delegation under the leadership of Sokolnikov[37] arrived....

2.2
Soviet Protest against Allied Intervention, June 27, 1918[38]

The following diplomatic note was issued by the Soviet government in response to the landing of British forces, as part of the Allied anti-German war effort, in northern Russia's Murmansk region in March 1918. Georgii Chicherin (1872–1936), who laid the foundations of Soviet diplomacy, had just replaced Trotsky as Commissar of Foreign Relations.

By the will of the working people, cognizant of the unity of their interests and in solidarity with the working masses of the whole world, the Russian Socialist Federative Soviet Republic has quit the ranks of the belligerent powers and exited the state of war, which was impossible for Russia to maintain due to its internal condition.

The working people of Russia and the Worker-Peasant Government, which is implementing its will, only seek to live in peace and friendship with all other peoples. The working people of Russia do not threaten any people with war and could not be a source of any threat to Great Britain.

Therefore, the Worker-Peasant Government cannot refrain from protesting even more forcefully against the invasion of the English armed force, which arrived in Murmansk without any aggressive provocation from the Russian side.

The armed forces of the Russian Republic are charged with the task to protect the Murmansk region against any foreign intervention and the Soviet troops will carry out this obligation, unswervingly fulfilling its revolutionary duty to guard Soviet Russia to the end.

---

37. Grigorii Sokolnikov (1888–1939) replaced Trotsky as lead negotiator.

38. Source: *Iz istorii grazhdanskoi voiny v SSSR: Sbornik dokumentov i materialov v trekh tomakh*, 3 vols. (Moscow: Institut Marksa-Engel'sa-Lenina, 1960), 1:29–30.

The People's Commissariat of Foreign Affairs insists most decisively that no armed forces of Great Britain or of any other foreign power should be present in Murmansk, a city of a neutral Russia. The Commissariat repeats its numerously declared protestation against the presence of the English warships in the Murmansk harbor expressing at the same time its firm expectation that the government of Great Britain will retract this measure, which is contrary to Russia's international status, and that the working people of Russia, which ardently desires to maintain friendly and unperturbed relations with Great Britain, will not be involuntarily put in a situation incompatible with its most sincere aspirations.

2.3
Vladimir Lenin, "A Letter to American Workingmen," August 20, 1918[39]

The letter below was written by Vladimir Lenin (under the pseudonym N. Lenin) on August 20, 1918, marking the Bolsheviks' growing commitment to a global struggle for hearts and minds. A Bolshevik emissary Petr Ivanovich Travin (Sletov), an old Bolshevik, took the letter to the United States, along with a copy of the Soviet Constitution and a diplomatic note to Woodrow Wilson demanding an end to US intervention in Russia. The American journalist, John Reed (1887–1920), arranged for its publication in several American newspapers and magazines. By the end of the year a less strident version of the letter was published in The Class Struggle, *a socialist periodical. That version is excerpted below with the addition of the omitted sections translated from the Russian original and inserted in square brackets.*

* * *

39. Sources: N. Lenin, *A Letter to American Workingmen: From the Socialist Soviet Republic of Russia* (New York: The Socialist Publication Society, 1918), 3–4, 9–12, 14; and V. I. Lenin, "Pis'mo k amerikanskim rabochim," in *Polnoe sobranie sochinenii*, 5th ed., 55 vols. (Moscow: Gos. izd. politicheskoi literatury, 1958–1965), 37:48–49, 60.

The history of modern civilized America opens with one of those really revolutionary wars of liberation of which there have been so few compared with the enormous number of wars of conquest that were caused, like the present imperialistic war, by squabbles among kings, landholders, and capitalists over the division of ill-gotten lands and profits. It was a war of the American people against the English [brigands] who despoiled America of its resources and held it in colonial subjection, just as their "civilized" descendants are draining the lifeblood of hundreds of millions of human beings in India, Egypt, and all corners and ends of the world to keep them in subjection.

Since that war 150 years have passed. Bourgeois civilization has borne its most luxuriant fruit. By developing the productive forces of organized human labor, by utilizing machines and all the wonders of technique America has taken the first place among free and civilized nations. But at the same time America, like a few other nations, has become characteristic for the depth of the abyss that divide a handful of brutal millionaires who are stagnating in a mire of luxury, and millions of laboring starving men and women who are always staring want in the face. [The American people, who had given the world an example of a revolutionary war against feudal slavery, has fallen into the latest capitalist wage-slavery at the hands of a small circle of billionaires, has found itself playing the role of hired executioner, which for the benefit of the rich scum strangled the Philippines in 1898 under the pretext of its "liberation"[40] and in 1918 is strangling the Russian Socialist Federative Republic under the pretext of "defending" it against the Germans.]

* * *

We are accused of having brought devastation upon Russia. Who is it that makes these accusations? The train-bearers of the bourgeoisie, of that same bourgeoisie that almost completely destroyed the culture of Europe, that has dragged the whole continent back to barbarism, that has brought hunger and destruction to the world. This bourgeoisie now demands that we find a different basis for our Revolution than that of destruction, that we shall not build it up upon the ruins of war, with

---

40. The reference is to the Spanish-American War, when the United States seized the Philippines and, following a bloody anti-insurgency campaign, subjugated the country.

human beings degraded and brutalized by years of warfare. O, how human, how just is this bourgeoisie!

* * *

The bourgeoisie of international imperialism has succeeded in slaughtering 10 millions, in crippling 20 millions in its war [in order to settle which predators, the English or the Germans, will rule the world]. Should our war, the war of the oppressed and the exploited, against oppressors and exploiters, cost a half or a whole million victims in all countries, the bourgeoisie would still maintain that the victims of the world war died a righteous death, that those of the civil war were sacrificed for a criminal cause.

* * *

Let the corrupt bourgeois press trumpet every mistake that is made by our Revolution out into the world. We are not afraid of our mistakes. The beginning of the revolution has not sanctified humanity. It is not to be expected that the working classes who have been exploited and forcibly held down by the clutches of want, of ignorance and degradation for centuries should conduct its revolution without mistakes. The dead body of bourgeois society cannot simply be put into a coffin and buried. It rots in our midst, poisons the air we breathe, pollutes our lives, clings to the new, the fresh, the living with a thousand threads and tendrils of old customs, of death and decay.

But for every hundred of our mistakes that are heralded into the world by the bourgeoisie and its sycophants, there are ten thousand great deeds of heroism, greater and more heroic because they seem so simple and unpretentious, because they take place in the everyday life of the factory districts or in secluded villages, because they are the deeds of people who are not in the habit of proclaiming their every success to the world, who have no opportunity to do so.

But even if the contrary were true,—I know, of course, that this is not so—but even if we had committed 10,000 mistakes to every 100 wise and righteous deeds, yes, even then our revolution would be great and invincible. And it will go down in the history of the world as unconquerable. For the first time in the history of the world not the minority, not alone the rich and the educated, but the real masses, the huge majority of the working-class itself, are building up a new world, are deciding the most difficult questions of social organization from out of their own experience.

* * *

We know that it may take a long time before help can come from you, comrades, American Workingmen, for the development of the revolution in the different countries proceeds along various paths, with varying rapidity (how could it be otherwise)! We know full well that the outbreak of the European proletarian revolution may take many weeks to come, quickly as it is ripening in these days. We are counting on the inevitability of the international revolution. But that does not mean that we count upon its coming at some definite, nearby date. We have experienced two great revolutions in our own country, that of 1905 and that of 1917, and we know that revolutions can come neither at a word of command, nor according to prearranged plans. We know that circumstances alone have pushed us, the proletariat of Russia, forward, that we have reached this new stage in the social life of the world not because of our superiority but because of the peculiarly reactionary character of Russia. But until the outbreak of the international revolution, revolutions in individual countries may still meet with a number of serious setbacks and overthrows.

* * *

We are in a beleaguered fortress, so long as no other international socialist revolution comes to our assistance with its armies. But these armies exist, they are stronger than ours, they grow, they strive, they become more invincible the longer imperialism with its brutalities continues. Workingmen the world over are breaking with their betrayers, with their Gompers and their Scheidemanns.[41] Inevitably labor is approaching communistic Bolshevistic tactics, is preparing for the proletarian revolution that alone is capable of preserving culture and humanity from destruction.

We are invincible, for invincible is the Proletarian Revolution.

---

41. Samuel Gompers (1850–1924) was the founder and longest-serving president of the American Federation of Labor (AFL). Philipp Scheidemann (1865–1939) was a leader of the Social Democratic Party of Germany (SPD).

2.4
Pitfalls of Intervention, 1918–1920[42]

*The first document below is an excerpt from an informal dip-
lomatic message sent by US Secretary of State Robert Lansing
(1864–1928), on July 17, 1918, to the Allied ambassadors articu-
lating a justification for intervention in Russia. Maj. Gen. William
S. Graves, commander of the US Expeditionary Force in Siberia,
received a copy of the message from Secretary of War Newton
Baker, Jr. (1871–1937). The second document is Graves's pes-
simistic report, filed on June 30, 1920, concerning the status of
Allied intervention forces and the general political and economic
conditions he observed in Russia.*

Document 1

The whole heart of the people of the United States is in the winning
of this war. The controlling purpose of the Government of the United
States is to do everything that is necessary and effective to win it....

* * *

In such circumstances it feels it to be its duty to say that it cannot, so long
as the military situation on the western front remains critical, consent to
break or slacken the force of its present effort by diverting any part of its
military force to other points and objectives....

* * *

It is the clear and fixed judgment of the Government of the United
States, arrived at after repeated and very searching re-considerations of
the whole situation in Russia that military intervention there would add

---

42. Sources: Document 1: US Department of State, *Foreign Relations of the United
States, 1918, Russia II* (1932), 287–89; Document 2: NARA, RG 395.9, Historical
Files of the AEF in Siberia, Final report of Maj. Gen. William S. Graves on the opera-
tions of AEF in Siberia, July 1, 1919–Mar. 30, 1920. Roll 10, file 21-33.6.

to the present sad confusion in Russia rather than cure it, injure rather than help her, and that it would be of no advantage in the prosecution of our main design, to win the war against Germany, it cannot, therefore, take part in such intervention, or sanction it in principle. Military intervention would, in its judgment, even supposing it to be efficacious in its immediate avowed object of delivering an attack upon Germany from the East, be merely a method of making use of Russia, not a method of serving her.... Whether from Vladivostok, or from Murmansk and Archangel, the only legitimate object for which American or allied troops can be employed, it submits, is to guard military stores which may subsequently be needed by Russian forces and to render such aid as may be acceptable to the Russians in the organization of their own self-defense. For helping the Czecho-Slovaks[43] there is immediate necessity and sufficient justification. Recent developments have made it evident that that is in the interest of what the Russian people themselves desire, and the Government of the United States is glad to contribute the small force at its disposal for that purpose....

* * *

Document 2

* * *

The people soon found that the troops of foreign governments were guarding the railroad for the benefit of Kolchak,[44] and not for the benefit of the people. This naturally resulted in a resentment of the people, not only against the Kolchak government, but against the Allied Forces engaged in guarding the railroad.

This is the only case where the action of American Corps could be considered as taking sides and justifying a resentment of a certain action of the Russian people against the United States.

---

43. On the Czechoslovak Legion, see Historical Essay, p. 34.

44. Aleksandr Kolchak (1874–1920) was a polar explorer, commander in the Imperial Russian Navy, and leader of anti-Bolshevik forces in Eastern Russia.

Notwithstanding the assistance we were giving the Kolchak government, the fact that I would not send troops out of the railroad sector to look for anti-Kolchak troops and disperse them, caused great criticism from the Kolchak adherents.

When the railroad employees refused work, it was generally stated their action was due to political convictions, and many of them would be arrested by the Kolchak authorities. The pay of these workmen was not such, during a great part of the time we were guarding the railroad, to even subsist the workman himself, let alone his family, if he had one. The value of the rouble fluctuated from about ten cents to less than one fourth of a cent. The average pay of the railroad employees, when the rouble was selling at two hundred and fifty for one American dollar, was less than three dollars a month, and I have been informed that many of these workmen had nothing but tea and bread for months.

* * *

My belief is the result of intervention in Siberia is going to be very harmful to the United States, Japan, England, and France, but less so to the United States than to the others....

...There is no question that the people, or ninety percent of the people, were outrageously treated by the Kolchak representatives. They were robbed, beaten, exploited and thousands murdered by men who professed to be supporting Kolchak....It was a common statement of representatives of all classes, except the Kolchak government class, that the treatment of the people was worse than in the time of the Czar....

* * *

...Ninety percent of the people of Russia, including in Siberia, are composed of peasants and workmen. These people, since the beginning of the war in 1914, have not only undergone great suffering, but have experienced great losses of men and property. They are all tired of war. They are more desirous of peace than of any other one thing in the world....The Soviet Government has evidently convinced the people of Siberia that their form of government offers an opportunity for restoration of peaceful conditions....

* * *

2.5
Bolshevik Anticipation of a
Revolutionary Wave in 1919[45]

Mikhail Voronkov (1893–1973) was a Bolshevik and leading Soviet official in Riazan province. He was attending the 8th Party Congress when news of the Hungarian Revolution reached Moscow. The following excerpts from his diary record excitement as well as eager anticipation of new revolutions erupting across Europe—feelings shared throughout the Bolshevik Party.

18 March [1919].

* * *

Last night comrade Lenin opened the congress in the Kremlin....Lenin talked about the international situation, arguing that we need to view the Entente countries as no different than German imperialism, which is why the Soviet government is ready to accept even the most unfavorable conditions, if only peace can be concluded.[46]

* * *

22 March [1919].

* * *

During the evening session, Bukharin barged into the Presidium, jumping and leaping around, and began explaining something to the people around him. Confusion followed. It turned out that Lenin had been contacted via wireless transmission from Budapest—in Hungary power

---

45. Source: Mikhail I. Voronkov, *Intelligent i epokha: Dnevniki, vospominaniia, stat'i, 1911–1941 gg.*, ed. A. O. Nikitin (Riazan': NRIID, 2013), 128, 130, 135, 139, 141. The editors are grateful to Gleb Albert for bringing this book to our attention.

46. Lenin was referring to the Paris Peace Conference, which met from January 1919 to January 1920.

shifted to the Communists. The Congress applauded for a long time after the announcement and welcomed a Hungarian Communist[47] who made a speech.

* * *

5 April [1919]. Work's little nuisances are hurtfully unnerving. Everyone comes to see me asking for everything: boots and soap, timber and woolen cloth, and kerosene! I really can't wait to be done with this work in the City Executive Committee, since I am in such a state sometimes that I am ready to beat up everybody...Lyriev,[48] from the Provincial Party Committee, presented a report on the struggle with the enemies of Soviet power. For the purpose of defending socialism, it is necessary to insinuate secret informers among the SRs[49]—this is disgusting, but obviously unavoidable: the countryside is turning restive again, as in the fall, because of the official grain inventory.[50] I wish the workers' revolution in Germany and France would come soon. It hurts so much to be waiting!

* * *

21 April [1919].
...There was a radio report on the revolution in Turkey[51] and the establishment of Soviets there. What joy! Now the Black Sea campaign of the Allies will be lost and so will their fleet and landing forces. One can now breath easier, in the assurance of the great inevitable cause of world revolution...

* * *

---

47. Endre Rudnianskii (1884?–?) was a Hungarian lawyer and Communist activist.

48. Nikita Lyriev (1893–?) then headed both the Cheka and the Revolutionary Tribunal in the city of Riazan.

49. The Socialist-Revolutionary Party was traditionally the most popular political party among the peasantry.

50. The grain inventory was conducted for the purpose of calculating obligatory deliveries to the state.

51. The author is referring to the initial developments of the Turkish War of Independence (May 1919–July 1923).

2–22 May [1919].

A whirlwind of events in the past twenty days. Party and Soviet life is in full swing, centering on the question of the struggle against Kolchak. We are sending convoys [of troops] and holding political rallies, with the deepest conviction that truth and victory belong to us. The Allies are traitors, and the majority of Western socialists are has-beens! How the whole world would glow with red flames, if in at least one of the Entente countries a worker revolution would break out!...

All these days I dealt with matters of city administration. It took a lot of effort to compel the department of communal services to tidy up the city; the question of fuel is worrisome; [state] procurement of [firewood] has almost halted,[52] and one cannot face winter relying solely on the Provincial Forest Committee....

* * *

2.6
Report of the Chief of the International Relations Section of the Comintern, March 1, 1921[53]

The Bolshevik leaders subsidized and controlled the Comintern throughout its existence. They aimed to advance the work of Communist parties and to encourage their efforts to foment revolution, as this report by a senior Comintern official indicates.

To the Chairman of the Executive Committee of Comintern (IKKI), Comrade Zinoviev

Copy to the General Secretary

---

52. Such procurements were often coerced, sometimes performed by "hostages" taken among politically suspect groups, and nearly always on terms disadvantageous to those making deliveries to the state.

53. Source: Daly and Trofimov, eds., *Russia in War and Revolution*, 201–2.

During my trip I visited the following countries: POLAND, CZECHOSLOVAKIA, AUSTRIA, ITALY, GERMANY, LITHU-ANIA, and LATVIA. I will present my proposals about these countries in that order.

I. POLAND

The Polish Communist Party is the only large illegal party close-ly linked to the masses. It has a strong influence on the working class....It has almost no income and is forced to live entirely at the expense of the IKKI. The needs of the party are many. Until October 15, 1921, they received from us 1,000,000 German marks per month, and after that date, because of a change in the exchange rate, nearly double that amount.

* * *

II. CZECHOSLOVAKIA

* * *

Here is my proposal in terms of financing the Czech Communist Party: provide substantial assistance as a loan for organizational ex-penses and for newspapers to prevent their press from collapsing; also this year allocate a certain amount for waging their electoral campaign for parliament; they will need a large amount, since the bourgeois parties will be fighting hard against them.

* * *

III. AUSTRIA

... the Austrian Communist Party does not constitute a revolution-ary base, nor does it stand up to the military cliques seeking to attack Russia.... yet cutting off subsidies threatens the closure of [their] newspaper...

My proposal is to purchase a printing press for publishing *Die Rote Fane*...under the condition that it would not be given to the party but would remain a private enterprise under the control of the IKKI....

IV. ITALY

...I think it is a mistake that the party does not allow its members to join pan-proletarian organizations that combat the fascists. The working masses are much angered by fascism, and this mood could be used for communist propaganda and for unifying workers in the struggle against the fascists....

The party lives entirely at the expense of Comintern and has no hopes for independent existence. Their only available revenue is 50,000 party cards at 5 lire each per year for a total of 250,000 lire. By contrast, the expenses for the central apparatus and subsidies to local organizations alone add up to 733,200 lire per year. If one adds to this 240,000 lire for illegal work and 100,000 for relations with other parties, then, together with expenses for their newspapers and publishing operations, the grand total reaches 4,306,000 lire, which under the current circumstances we are absolutely unable to provide.

* * *

V. GERMANY

* * *

Concerning the financing of the Communist Party of Germany, the Party itself seeks to receive less assistance from Comintern but cannot do without it entirely. Still, it is possible to reduce this assistance without damaging the work of the Communist Party. They can reduce the central apparatus and terminate newspaper subsidies for local organizations.

Director of the Department of International Relations of the IKKI

2.7
Toward World Revolution, July 3, 1921[54]

When the Third Congress of the Comintern met in Moscow in summer 1921, the prospects for an international communist revolution looked bleak compared to 1919. Yet, by now the Bolshevik government had won the Civil War. Below is an excerpt from the resolution "On Tactics," which takes into account these new realities. It spells out the tactics Communist parties should pursue to achieve their objectives: overthrowing capitalism, setting up a proletarian dictatorship, and creating "an international Soviet republic."

3. The Important Task of the Present

In view of these imminent new struggles, the question of the attainment of decisive influence on the most important sections of the working class, in short, the leadership of the struggle, is the most important question now confronting the Third International. For, despite the present objective revolutionary economic and political situation wherein the acutest revolutionary crisis may arise suddenly (whether in the form of a big strike, or a colonial upheaval, or a new war, or even a severe parliamentary crisis) the majority of the working class is not yet under the influence of Communism. Particularly is this true in such countries, as for example, England and America, where large strata of workers depending for their existence on the power of finance capital are corrupted by imperialism, and the real revolutionary propaganda among the masses has only just begun....

* * *

---

54. Source: *Theses and Resolutions Adopted at the Third World Congress of the Communist International (June 22nd–July 12th, 1921)* (New York: The Contemporary Publishing Association, 1921), 38, 51, 54–55, 58–59, 60–61, 63, 65–66.

[6.] Broadening the Fight

* * *

The character of the transition period makes it imperative for all Communist Parties to be thoroughly prepared for the struggle. Each separate struggle may lead to the struggle for power. Preparedness can only be achieved by giving to the entire Party agitation the character of a vehement attack against capitalist society. The Party must also come into contact with the widest masses of workers, and must make it plain to them that they are being led by a vanguard, whose real aim is—the conquest of power. The Communist press and proclamations must not merely consist of theoretical proofs that Communism is right. They must be clarion calls of the proletarian revolution. The parliamentary activity of the Communists must not consist in debates with the enemy, or in attempts to convert him, but in the ruthless unmasking of the agents of the bourgeoisie and the stirring up of the fighting spirit of the working masses and in attracting the semi-proletarian and the petty bourgeois strata of society to the proletariat. Our organizing work in the trade-unions, as well as in the party organizations, must not consist in mechanically increasing the number of our membership. It must be imbued with the consciousness of the coming struggle. It is only in becoming, in all its forms and manifestations, the embodiment of the will to fight, that the Party will be able to fulfil its task, when the time for drastic action will have arrived.

* * *

8. The Forms and Means of Direct Action

* * *

In the course of the past year, during which we saw the ever increasing arrogance of the capitalist offensive against the workers, we observed that the bourgeoisie in all countries, not satisfied with the normal activity of its state organs, created legal and semi-legal though state-protected

White-Guard organizations, which played a decisive part in every big economic or industrial conflict.

* * *

The bourgeoisie, though apparently conscious of its power and actually bragging about its stability, knows through its leading governments quite well, that it has merely obtained a breathing spell and that under the present circumstances every big strike has the tendency to develop into civil war and the immediate struggle for the possession of power.

In the struggle of the proletariat against the capitalist offensive it is the duty of the Communists not only to take the advanced posts and lead those engaged in the struggle to a complete understanding of the fundamental revolutionary tasks, but it is also their duty, relying upon the best and most active elements among the workers, to create their own workers legions and militant organizations which would resist the pacifists and teach the "golden youth" of the bourgeoisie a wholesome lesson that will break them of the strike-breaking habit.

In view of the extraordinary importance of the counter-revolutionary shock-troops, the Communist Party must, through its nuclei in the unions, devote special attention to this question, organizing a thorough-going educational and communication service which shall keep under constant observation the military organs and forces of the enemy, his headquarters, his arsenals, the connection between these headquarters and the police, the press and the political parties, and work out all the necessary details of defense and counter-attack.

The Communist Party must in this manner convince the widest circles of the proletariat by word and deed that every economic or political conflict, given the necessary combination of circumstances, may develop into civil war, in the course of which it will become the task of the Proletariat to conquer the power of the state.

* * *

10. International Coordination of Action

* * *

...The unconditional support of Soviet Russia is still the main duty of the Communists of all countries. Not only must they act resolutely against any attacks on Soviet Russia, but they must also struggle to do away with all the obstacles placed by capitalist states in the way of Russia's communication with the world market and all other nations. Only if Soviet Russia succeeds in reconstructing economic life, in mitigating the terrible misery caused by the three years of imperialist war and three years of civil war, only when Soviet Russia will have contrived to raise the efficiency of the masses of its population, will it be in a position, in the future, to assist the western proletarian States with food and raw material, and protect them against being enslaved by American Capital. The International political task of the Communist International consists not in demonstrations on special occasions, but in the permanent increase of the international relations of the Communists, in their ceaseless struggle in closed formation. It is impossible to foretell at what front the proletariat will succeed in breaking the capitalist lines, whether it will be in capitalist Germany with its workers who are most cruelly oppressed by the German and the Entente bourgeoisie, and are faced by the alternative of either winning or dying, or in the agrarian southwest, or in Italy, where the decay of the bourgeoisie has reached an advanced stage. It is therefore the duty of the Communist International to intensify its efforts on all the sectors of the workers' world front, and it is the duty of the Communist Parties to support with all their means the decisive battles of each section of the Communist International. This must be achieved by immediately widening and deepening all international conflicts in every other country, as soon as a great struggle breaks out in any one country.

* * *

2.8
The Treaty of Rapallo, April 16, 1922[55]

*The Treaty of Rappalo stunned the other European governments —
as two "pariah states" drew closer in the face of Western hostility —
and represented a milestone in the Bolsheviks' growing embrace
of state diplomacy.*

German-Russian Agreement; April 16, 1922 (Treaty of Rapallo)

The German Government, represented by Dr. Walther Rathenau,[56]
Minister of State, and the Government of the Russian Socialist Federal
Soviet Republic, represented by M. Tchitcherin, People's Commissary,
have agreed upon the following provisions:

Article 1

The two Governments are agreed that the arrangements arrived at
between the German Reich and the Russian Socialist Federal Soviet
Republic, with regard to questions dating from the period of war between
Germany and Russia, shall be definitely settled upon the following basis:
   [a] The German Reich and the Russian Socialist Federal Soviet
Republic mutually agree to waive their claims for compensation for
expenditure incurred on account of the war, and also for war damages,
that is to say, any damages which may have been suffered by them and by
their nationals in war zones on account of military measures, including
all requisitions in enemy country. Both Parties likewise agree to forego
compensation for any civilian damages, which may have been suffered
by the nationals of the one Party on account of so-called exceptional war

---

55. Source: League of Nations, *Treaty Series; Publication of Treaties and International
Engagements Registered with the Secretariat of the League* (Geneva: League of Nations,
1923), vol. 19, pp. 248–52.

56. Walther Rathenau (1867–1922), a leading German industrialist and statesman,
was appointed Foreign Minister in January 1922. Rightwing conspirators murdered
him in June, in part for his role in negotiating the Rapallo Treaty.

measures or on account of emergency measures carried out by the other Party.

[b] Legal relations in public and private matters arising out of the state of war, including the question of the treatment of trading vessels which have fallen into the hands of either Party, shall be settled on a basis of reciprocity.

[c] Germany and Russia mutually agree to waive their claims for compensation for expenditure incurred by either party on behalf of prisoners of war. Furthermore the German Government agrees to forego compensation with regard to the expenditure incurred by it on behalf of members of the Red Army interned in Germany. The Russian Government agrees to forego the restitution of the proceeds of the sale carried out in Germany of the army stores brought into Germany by the interned members of the Red Army mentioned above.

Article 2

Germany waives all claims against Russia which may have arisen through the application, up to the present, of the laws and measures of the Russian Socialist Federal Soviet Republic to German nationals or their private rights and the rights of the German Reich and states, and also claims which may have arisen owing to any other measures taken by the Russian Socialist Federal Soviet Republic or by their agents against German nationals or the private rights, on condition that the government of the Russian Socialist Federal Soviet Republic does not satisfy claims for compensation of a similar nature made by a third Party.

Article 3

Diplomatic and consular relations between the German Reich and the Russian Socialist Federal Soviet Republic shall be resumed immediately. The conditions for the admission of the Consuls of both Parties shall be determined by means of a special agreement.

Article 4

Both Governments have furthermore agreed that the establishment of the legal status of those nationals of the one Party, which live within the territory of the other Party, and the general regulation of mutual, commercial and economic relations, shall be effected on the principle of the most favoured nation. This principle shall, however, not apply to the privileges and facilities which the Russian Socialist Federal Soviet Republic may grant to a Soviet Republic or to any State which in the past formed part of the former Russian Empire.

Article 5

The two Governments shall co-operate in a spirit of mutual goodwill in meeting the economic needs of both countries. In the event of a fundamental settlement of the above question on an international basis, an exchange of opinions shall previously take place between the two Governments. The German Government, having lately been informed of the proposed agreements of private firms, declares its readiness to give all possible support to these arrangements and to facilitate their being carried into effect.

Article 6

Articles 1[b] and 4 of this Agreement shall come into force on the day of ratification, and the remaining provisions shall come into force immediately.

Original text done in duplicate at Rapallo on April 16, 1922.

Signed: Rathenau

Signed: Tchitcherin

2.9

Joseph Stalin, "The Political Tasks of the University of the Toiling Peoples of the East," 1925[57]

Bolshevik leaders directly supervised and participated in the work of the international revolutionary universities instituted in the USSR beginning in 1921. On May 18, 1925, Joseph Stalin delivered a speech to a student meeting at the Communist University of the Toilers of the East, which by then already bore his name. In his speech, Stalin greeted "the sons of the East," yet he noted that the university's tasks of nation- and socialist state-building in the Soviet republics of the East were quite distinct from its tasks in the colonial and dependent countries of the East. The excerpt below reflects Stalin's thinking about the latter tasks.

* * *

From the foregoing, one can deduce at the very least the following three inferences:

1) To achieve the liberation of colonial and dependent countries from imperialism is impossible without victorious revolution. You cannot win independence for free.

2) It is impossible to move the revolution forward and to gain full independence in those colonies and dependent countries where capitalism is developed without isolating the collaborationist national bourgeoisie, without liberating the petty-bourgeois revolutionary masses from the influence of this bourgeoisie, without working toward the hegemony of the proletariat, without organizing the progressive elements of the working class into an independent communist party.

3) It is impossible to achieve a durable victory in colonial and dependent countries without a genuine alliance between the liberation movement of these countries and the proletarian movement of the advanced countries of the West.

---

57. Source: I. V. Stalin, *Sochineniia*, 18 vols. (Moscow: Gos. izd. politicheskoi literatury, 1946–1952), 7:133–52.

* * *

What are the immediate tasks of the revolutionary movement of the colonies and dependent countries in light of these circumstances? The key aspect of the nature of colonies and dependent countries at the present moment is that there is no longer any such thing as a single and all-encompassing East. In the past, the colonial East was represented as something unitary and homogenous. Today this view no longer reflects reality. There are now at least three categories of colonial and dependent countries. First, there are countries like Morocco, which have no or almost no proletariat and which are undeveloped in regard to industry. Second, there are countries like China and Egypt, whose industry is little developed industrially and whose proletariat is relatively small. Third, there are countries like India, which are fairly developed capitalistically and have a fairly numerous national proletariat.

Clearly it is not possible to place all such countries on the same level.

* * *

These tasks become particularly serious and significant if they are considered in light of the present international situation. The international situation at the moment is characterized by a temporary lull in the revolutionary movement. But what is a lull and what can it signify at the present moment? It can only signify growing pressure on the workers in the West, on the colonies of the East, and, above all, on the Soviet Union as the standard bearer of the revolutionary movement in all countries.... Therefore the question of preparing a counterstrike of the united forces of revolution against a likely strike from the imperialist camp is inescapably the order of the day.

That is why the unflinching fulfillment of the present tasks of the revolutionary movement in colonies and dependent countries has acquired especial importance at this moment.

* * *

One has to be aware of the existence of two deviations in the practical work of activists of the colonial East, which have to be fought against in order to successfully cultivate truly revolutionary cadres.

The first deviation is underestimating the revolutionary potential of the liberation movement and overestimating the idea of a united all-encompassing national front in colonies and dependent countries regardless of their conditions and extent of development. This deviation to the right threatens to undermine the revolutionary movement and to dissolve the communist elements in the wide-ranging choir of bourgeois nationalists. Decisive struggle against this deviation is the manifest obligation of the University of the Peoples of the East.

The second deviation is overestimating the revolutionary potential of the liberation movement and underestimating the goal of achieving a union of the working class and the revolutionary bourgeoisie against imperialism. This deviation, it seems, is afflicting Communists in Java who recently mistakenly adopted the motto of Soviet power for their country. This deviation to the left threatens to sunder the bonds with the masses of the Communist Party and to transform it into a sect. Decisive struggle against this deviation is the essential condition for cultivating truly revolutionary activists in the colonies and dependent countries of the East.

* * *

2.10
Bolshevik Influence in China, 1920s[58]

On June 26, 1927, the Chinese Communist Politburo met in joint session with representatives of the Executive Committee of the Comintern to discuss instructions recently sent from Moscow. The minutes of the session excerpted below reveal both the degree and the limits of Moscow's influence over the rapidly developing political situation in China.

* * *

---

58. Source: RGASPI, f. 514, op. 1, d. 298, ll. 69–72.

CHEN DUXIU:[59] We have two paths before us: one on the left and one on the right. The one on the right means giving up everything; the one on the left means radical actions. We will perish taking either path.

Besides, there is a middle path, i.e., the continuation of the present situation—this is also impossible.

So what can we do? Perhaps we should look for a fourth path? We need to discuss this at our session.

BORODIN:[60] First, we need to reach an agreement with Moscow. For six weeks we have been receiving cables conveying a particular view. We have disagreed with this view and have repeatedly expressed our disagreement to Moscow, which has insisted that we carry out its directives. The task is to find a new, common ground with Moscow.

(He then reads a cable from Moscow addressed to Wang Jingwei.[61]) The contents are basically as follows:

"In the present dangerous situation we consider it our revolutionary duty to declare to you the following: salvation is only in joining with the peasantry, not in confrontation with the peasantry. The Guomindang must understand that it is necessary to implement an agrarian revolution. Vacillation must stop. The Guomindang must more closely unite with the CP and together with it form a revolutionary power.[62] Besides, it is necessary to reorganize the Guomindang, to bring in new leaders from the working class and the peasantry. We must create a firm basis for the party, a firm revolutionary power."

...What does Moscow want? Moscow wants:

1) agrarian revolution,

2) democratization of the Guomindang (proletarization and the involvement of the peasantry),

---

59. Chen Duxiu (1879–1942) cofounded the Chinese Communist Party and served as its General Secretary from 1921 to 1927.

60. Mikhail Borodin (born Gruzenberg; 1884–1951) emigrated to the United States in 1906 and studied law and philosophy at Valparaiso University in Indiana. He returned to Russia in 1918. Lenin sent him to the USA and Mexico to promote the Comintern in 1919. In 1923, he was sent as a Comintern envoy CCP and a Soviet political advisor to the Guomindang. He helped forge an alliance between them.

61. Wang Jingwei (1883–1944) was then a leftist member of the Guomindang, closely associated with Mao Zedong, Chen Duxiu, and Borodin.

62. The word translated here as "power" in Russian is *vlast'*. It denotes variously government, leadership, power, and authority.

3) the creation of a revolutionary army,

4) not exiting the government and the Guomindang (which is viewed as reckless).

If we act in accordance with these four points, the issue of the party's independence will resolve itself; it will no longer be a problem.

(KHITAROV[63] shouts: Then the Communist party will lead.)

Yes, then the Communist party will be the leader.

How does Moscow understand these tasks and how do I understand them?

1) Agrarian revolution.

It is not by accident that Moscow has issued a demand for an agrarian revolution, and not the confiscation of land. Here we can find common ground. Confiscation of land is not the beginning, but the end of an agrarian revolution. We should begin with other steps. We should tell Moscow what we mean by an agrarian revolution. We should determine whether Moscow means the same thing or it is demanding the immediate confiscation of land....

* * *

2) Democratization of the Guomindang.

Here there are two options. The first is to engage workers and peasants, to hold conferences in the provinces, to put out demands to renew the Guomindang from below.

The second is to advise the Guomindang to elect new leaders from the masses.

We must clearly tell the Comintern that the first option is possible, but the second option is impossible. The second option would inevitably provoke a break-up with the Guomindang....

3) Arming the workers and peasants.

This, of course, we welcome wholeheartedly. The situation, however, is such that we will not be able to remain in Wuhan for more than two months. What are our choices? Either we leave for Nanking, but there Feng[64] could attack us. In that case, we would probably have to retreat to Guangdong. We will have to surrender Wuhan in any case. Or we will

---

63. Rafael Khitarov (1900–1939) was an official of the Komsomol and of the Communist Youth International.

64. Feng Yuxiang (1882–1948) was a Chinese warlord allied with Chiang Kai-shek.

have to go underground together with the left Guomindang. But for this reason arming the workers and peasants is now practically impossible....
    4) Exiting the government.
    Moscow calls this a risky adventure. But we, that is, some of the comrades here, are even more radical than Moscow. They want to resign. But I think that here we can reach an agreement without much difficulty. It is not yet time to resign. We must remain in the government. This, of course, does not mean that every minister must actually remain in his office and work. He could designate his deputy, or his secretary, to remain and go abroad himself for six months if he desires. This is a technical issue. But as a political gesture, we must remain in the government, symbolically, as it were.

* * *

CHEN DUXIU: I do not understand Moscow directives and I cannot agree with them. Moscow simply does not understand what is going on here.... We know precisely what Moscow means by agrarian revolution. Moscow is demanding the confiscation of land, which we cannot accept.
    So Borodin's entire platform is nonsense.
    TAN PINGSHAN:[65] I do not agree with Chen Duxiu. I think we should accept Borodin's five points. To that end, we should cable Moscow once again. We should not exit the government. First, we, the Chinese, should determine our platform and only then notify Moscow about it.
    ZHANG GUOTAO:[66] I also think that Moscow's directives are unacceptable. We should reject them and notify Moscow about it. If Moscow continues to insist on its point of view, then we should send a cable in response and take a stand against Moscow.

* * *

---

65. Tan Pingshan (1886–1956) was a member of the Politburo of the CCP, head of the Central Peasant Department in the Wuhan government, a senior official of the Comintern, and a close associate of Borodin.

66. Zhang Guotao (1897–1979) was a founding member of the CCP and a rival to Mao.

ZHOU ENLAI:[67] In Shanghai, we received an order from Moscow to create a democratic government. Then, when we did it, we were told this was wrong. Moscow always acts this way. We should clarify what Moscow actually wants.

ZHANG TAILEI:[68] Since Roy[69] arrived, since the Comintern delegation was here, we have had constant disagreements. It all began with the Northern Expedition.[70] This situation is intolerable. We really need to come to an agreement.

We argued with the Comintern representative.[71] But when we asked him what he wanted to propose, on Sunday he wanted a demonstration, and on Wednesday, a strike. We cannot implement this. These demands are impossible to carry out.

KHITAROV then had a private talk with Borodin (while the session continued). He quoted Lenin to him, to the effect that those who assert that in revolutionary times, when civil war has already begun, we can engage only in propaganda and agitation and not in action, that those who reject action are either dead men or traitors to the revolution.

BORODIN said that this is generally speaking correct. At the current moment, these things cannot be separated.

* * *

---

67. Zhou Enlai (1898–1976) was, at the time, a member of the Politburo of the CCP.

68. Zhang Tailei (1898–1927) was a leader of the failed communist uprising in December 1927 in Guangzhou (then called Canton in English).

69. Born in India, Manabendra Roy (1887–1954) was a Comintern leader.

70. The Northern Expedition was a Guomindang military campaign in 1926–1928, which reunified China.

71. That is, Manabendra Roy.

2.11
Fighting over the Torch of the Revolution: Trotsky versus Stalin[72]

Trotsky's article, later known as "The Transitional Program," was adopted by the founding conference of the Fourth International, which met in September 1938 outside Paris. Trotsky's supporters embraced it as a roadmap for an international communist revolution.

The Death Agony of Capitalism and the Tasks of the Fourth International

The Objective Prerequisites for a Socialist Revolution

The world political situation as a whole is chiefly characterized by a historical crisis of the leadership of the proletariat.

The economic prerequisite for the proletarian revolution has already in general achieved the highest point of fruition that can be reached under capitalism. Mankind's productive forces stagnate. Already, new inventions and improvements fail to raise the level of material wealth. Conjunctural crises under the weight of the social crisis affecting the whole capitalist system impose ever heavier deprivations and sufferings upon the masses. Growing unemployment, in its turn, deepens the financial crisis of the State and undermines the unstable monetary systems. Democratic regimes, as well as fascist, stagger on from one bankruptcy to another.

The bourgeoisie itself sees no way out. In countries where it has already been forced to stake its last upon the card of fascism, it now toboggans with closed eyes toward an economic and military catastrophe. In the historically privileged countries, i.e., in those where the bourgeoisie can still for a certain period permit itself the luxury of democracy

---

72. Source: Leon Trotsky, "The Death Agony of Capitalism and the Tasks of the Fourth International," *Socialist Appeal*, vol. 2, no. 46 (October 22, 1938): 7.

at the expense of national accumulations (Great Britain, France, United States, etc.) all of capital's traditional parties are in a state of perplexity, bordering on a paralysis of will. The "New Deal," despite its first period of pretentious resoluteness, represents but a special form of political perplexity, possible only in a country where the bourgeoisie succeeded in accumulating incalculable wealth. The present crisis, far from having run its full course, has already succeeded in showing that "New Deal" politics, like Popular Front politics in France, opens no new exit from the economic blind alley.

International relations present no better picture. Under the increasing tension of capitalist disintegration, imperialist antagonisms reach an impasse at the height of which separate clashes and bloody local disturbances (Ethiopia, Spain, the Far East, Central Europe) must inevitably coalesce into a conflagration of world dimensions. The bourgeoisie, of course, is aware of the mortal danger to its domination represented by a new war. But that class is now immeasurably less capable of averting war than on the eve of 1914.

All talk to the effect that historical conditions have not yet "ripened" for socialism is the product of ignorance or conscious deception. The objective prerequisites for the proletarian revolution have not only "ripened"; they have begun to get somewhat rotten. Without a socialist revolution, in the next historical period at that—a catastrophe threatens the whole culture of mankind. The turn is now to the proletariat, i.e., chiefly to its revolutionary vanguard. The historical crisis of mankind is reduced to the crisis of the revolutionary leadership.

The Proletariat and Its Leadership

The economy, the state, the politics of the bourgeoisie and its international relations are completely blighted by a social crisis, characteristic of a pre-revolutionary state of society. The chief obstacle in the path of transforming the pre-revolutionary into a revolutionary state is the opportunist character of proletarian leadership; its petty bourgeois cowardice before the big bourgeoisie and its perfidious connection with it even in its death agony.

In all countries, the proletariat is wracked by a deep disquiet. In millions, the masses again and again move onto the road of revolutionary outbreaks. But each time they are blocked by their own conservative bureaucratic apparatus.

The Spanish proletariat has made a series of heroic attempts since April 1931 to take power in its hands and guide the fate of society. However, its own parties (Social Democrats, Stalinists, anarchists, POUMists[73])—each in its own way—acted as a brake and thus prepared Franco's[74] triumphs.

In France, the great wave of "sit-down" strikes, particularly during June 1936, revealed the wholehearted readiness of the proletariat to overthrow the capitalist system. However, the leading organizations (Socialists, Stalinists, Syndicalists) under the label of the Popular Front succeeded in channeling and damming, at least temporarily, the revolutionary stream.

The unprecedented wave of sit-down strikes and the amazingly rapid growth of industrial unionism in the United States (the CIO) is a most indisputable expression of the instinctive striving of the American workers to raise themselves to the level of the tasks imposed on them by history. But here, too, the leading political organizations, including the newly created CIO, do everything possible to keep in check and paralyze the revolutionary pressure of the masses.

The definite passing over of the Comintern to the side of the bourgeois order, its cynically counterrevolutionary role throughout the world, particularly in Spain, France, the United States, and other "democratic" countries, created exceptional supplementary difficulties for the world proletariat. Under the banner of the October Revolution, the conciliatory politics practiced by the "People's Front" dooms the working class to impotence and clears the road for fascism.

"People's Fronts" on the one hand—fascism on the other; these are the last political resources of imperialism in the struggle against the proletarian revolution. From the historical point of view, however, both these resources are stopgaps. The decay of capitalism continues under the sign of the Phrygian cap[75] in France as under the sign of the swastika in Germany. Nothing short of the overthrow of the bourgeoisie can open a road out.

---

73. Members of the Workers' Party of Marxist Unification, and independent Spanish Communist party.

74. Francisco Franco (1892–1975), a Spanish general, led a bloody civil war against the leftist Popular Front government, which came to power after the election of 1936, and then ruled as dictator of Spain from 1939 until 1975.

75. A symbol of liberty during the French Revolution of 1789–1794.

The orientation of the masses is determined first by the objective conditions of decaying capitalism, and second, by the treacherous politics of the old workers' organizations. Of these factors, the first, of course, is the decisive one: the laws of history are stronger than the bureaucratic apparatus. No matter how the methods of the social-betrayers differ—from the "social" legislation of Blum[76] to the judicial frame-ups of Stalin—they will never succeed in breaking the revolutionary will of the proletariat. As time goes on, their desperate efforts to hold back the wheel of history will demonstrate more clearly to the masses that the crisis of the proletarian leadership, having become the crisis in mankind's culture, can be resolved only by the Fourth International.

* * *

---

76. Léon Blum (1872–1950) was the socialist Prime Minister of France in a Popular Front government in 1936–1937.

Section 3
The Russian Revolution and the Power of Communism

3.1
John Reed on the Revolution and Socialism, 1919[77]

In the article "A New Appeal," published upon his return from Soviet Russia to the United States, John Reed critically evaluated the views of American workers and offered a strategy to engage them in the worldwide revolutionary movement.

It is time for American Socialists to do a little painful thinking. For my own satisfaction I should like to set down here what I think about the American Socialist Movement.

From my observations in different parts of the country, I should say that, roughly, the American Socialist Party is composed of two main elements:

1) American petty bourgeois (clerks, shopkeepers, administrative officers of small business, a few farmers); and American intellectuals (journalists, mainly).

2) Foreign-born workers; foreign-born intellectuals.

The most significant facts in the American Labor Movement are the American Federation of Labor and the I.W.W.[78] These two organizations prove that political Socialism has very little attraction for the American workingman; in fact, they prove that the American workman is *opposed* to Socialism.

Why?

---

77. Source: *The Revolutionary Age* (Boston), vol. 1, no. 14 (January 18, 1919): 8.

78. The Industrial Workers of the World (IWW), a radical labor union, was founded in 1905.

Let us consider first the American Federation of Labor. This is a purely economic organization, whose power consists in the fact that it *defends* certain workers against the assaults of the capitalist class, which by raising the cost of living and depressive relative wages, is always attempting to reduce the working class to the condition of peonage. Above all, men who work with their hands are *practical*, and the American Federation of Labor offers a practical program.

By reason of the history of this country, its boundless lands and natural resources, the stupendous growth of its cities, the immeasurable opportunities presented for energetic individuals in the immense demand for food, manufactured goods, and means of transportation, and the fluidity of social boundaries, the American worker has always believed, consciously or unconsciously, that he can become a millionaire or an eminent statesman. This is expressed in the saying, once heard often but now less frequently that "any American boy can be President." . . .

The American worker knows that this country is owned and controlled by "the Trusts." But he does not realize that the day of universal opportunity has passed. He believes, consciously or unconsciously, that he can still rise above the working class, and above his fellows. And because *many thousands* believe this, their unanimous sentiment is opposed to any system, like Socialism, which wishes to destroy their imagined opportunity. . . .

Moreover, although the American worker is profoundly disgusted with the dominant Democratic or Republican Parties, and if you ask him what he thinks of such-and-such a political candidate, will say, "Oh, he's just a dirty politician. They're all alike—they make promises, but they never do anything when they get elected"; although the American worker knows that Congress, the State Legislatures, and the City Councils are used by business interests for their own selfish purposes—still he does not know how to answer when he is told, "Well, if you don't like your officials, vote for somebody you *do* like. You are the boss. This is a free country."

The American worker still thinks *politically* instead of *economically*. No one has ever been able to tell him, in a way which he understands, that in our state of society the vote is almost powerless. As I have said, he knows that the men he elects to political office are dominated by Big Business after they get elected; but he doesn't realize that unless he, *the worker*, takes away *the power* of Big Business before he elects his representatives, those representatives will always be bought—or if they are honest, they will always be powerless.

Why doesn't the American worker vote the Socialist ticket? In the first place, he probably doesn't like Socialism, which means to him only a system worked out in foreign countries, not born of his own particular needs and opposed to "democracy" and "fair play," which is the way he has been taught to characterize the institutions of this country. In the second place, if he has become conscious of his *class* interests, voting for the Socialist Party seems to him *impractical*. "They won't win," he says, "it will just be 'throwing away my vote.'"

Of course he does not see that voting for a candidate who promises and does not perform is just as much "throwing away his vote" as voting the Socialist ticket.

Sometimes, however, the candidate *does* perform his promises; sometimes the popular discontent *does* force a legislative body to pass some needed social measures. The worker is satisfied; he does not follow the law to its most important stage—its operation. He does not watch the Courts which interpret the law. For example, take the various Anti-Injunction[79] bills which have passed Congress, hailed by the American Federation of Labor as "a new Magna Carta." And yet injunctions are still used as weapons against the workers in industrial disputes....Consider the Child Labor Law,[80] declared unconstitutional by the Supreme Court. The list of cleverly drawn and inefficient labor laws in the statute books is endless....And if the laws, as sometimes happens, are effective, the employers simply refuse to obey them, and drag out litigation in the courts until the whole matter is quietly forgotten.

The American worker does not see to the heart of the society in which he lives. When the truth becomes too obvious, he is easily persuaded that all abuses can be corrected by agitation, by the law, by the ballot box. He does not see that *the whole complex structure of our civilization is corrupt from top to bottom*, because the capitalist class controls the sources of wealth.

And yet there is one important truth which he has learned. He knows that the immediate problems of his daily life in industry cannot be solved by politics. For this is necessary a kind of insurrection—direct action—the strike....

* * *

---

79. Laws giving labor unions and organizers various legal protections.

80. Reed was referring to the Keating-Owen Child Labor Act of 1916.

If anything were needed to demonstrate the value of political action, the Russian Revolution ought to do it. No true Socialist denies that the parliament of the future Socialist State will be an Industrial parliament; but the transformation from the political to the industrial system must be expressed by political action, whose value in the class struggle lies in the fact that it *creates opportunities* for the education of the workers, and for industrial direct action, and *protects* these two essential methods of the struggle of the working class for power.

...

...My idea is to make Socialists, and there is only one way of doing that—by teaching Socialism, straight Socialism, revolutionary Socialism, international Socialism. This is what the Russian Bolsheviki did; this is what the German Spartacus group did. They approached not Socialists, but *people*: workers, peasants, soldiers, who did not know what Socialism was. First, they found out from the working people what they wanted most. Then they made those wants into an immediate program and explained how they were related to the other demands of the complete Social Revolution. And they explained, explained, eternally explained...

Revolutionary Socialism is not a refined theory adapted to cultivated minds. There is no value in inventing new Socialist tactics merely so that intellectuals can discuss what Karl Marx would have thought about it. Revolutionary Socialism, above all other kinds, must be *practical*—it must *work*—it must make *Socialists* out of workers and make them quick.

Comrades who call themselves "members of the Left Wing" have an immediate job to do. They must find out from *American workers* what they want most, and they must explain this in terms of the whole Labor Movement, and they must make the workers want more—make them want the whole Revolution.

* * *

And finally, the workers must be told that *they have the force*, if they will only organize it and express it; that if together they are able to stop work, no power in the universe can prevent them from doing what they want to do—if only they know what they want to do!

And it is our business to formulate what they want to do.

Said Nikolai Lenin[81] at the Peasants' Congress in Petrograd,[82] "If Socialism can only be realized when the intellectual development of all the people permits it, then we shall not see Socialism for at least five hundred years...The Socialist political party—this is the vanguard of the working class; it must not allow itself to be halted by the lack of education of the mass average, but it must lead the masses, relying upon the Labor Organizations for revolutionary initiative..."

And again, at the Third Congress of Soviets,[83] "You accuse us of using force...We admit it. All Government is legalized force, controlled by one class and used against another. For the first time in history, we in this hall are creating a legalized force controlled by the working class, the vast majority of the people, and directed against those who have exploited us and enslaved us..."

3.2
"Russia Did It," 1919[84]

The leaflet below, which circulated in Seattle during the strike of 1919, called upon workers to seize control of the shipyards, take their efforts to the national level, and carry out a revolutionary transformation on the Russian model. Although this strategy did not gain traction in the General Strike Committee or among the majority of workers, it shaped the conservative perception of the strike as the work of "domestic Bolshevism."

---

81. Nikolai Lenin was a pseudonym of Vladimir Lenin.

82. This congress took place in late November 1917.

83. The Third All-Russian Congress of Soviets of Workers', Soldiers' and Peasants' Deputies met in January 1918.

84. Source: Leaflet, Industrial Workers of the World, Seattle Office, Records. Industrial Workers of the World, Acc. 544, Box 3. Courtesy Labor Archives of Washington, University of Washington Libraries Special Collections.

3.3
Bela Kun, "Discipline and Centralized Leadership," 1923[85]

When Bela Kun published the article excerpted below, the Hungarian Soviet Republic's brief existence had ended. Its failure only reinforced his belief that centralism, discipline, and carefully planned strategy were key to the success of future communist revolutions.

* * *

I do not intend to enlarge upon the international and internal political causes which were favorable to the Russian Revolution, and which, on

85. Source: *The Communist Review*, Special Double Number, vol. 3, nos. 9 and 10 (January–February 1923): 469, 470, 471–73, 474.

the other hand, were detrimental to the Hungarian revolution. I shall only point to the fact that in Hungary we failed to provide, not only what Comrade Lenin described as a plan of retreat, but even a line of retreat. In regard to the Russian Revolution, I think that the circumstance which has belied all the Thermidor[86] prophesies about Soviet Russia was the following:—In Russia there was a centralized, disciplined and self-sacrificing Workers' Party in the shape of the Russian Communist Party. The absence of such a Party or of anything approaching it in Hungary was the cause of the inevitable collapse of the proletarian revolution, notwithstanding all the sacrifices and enthusiasm of the Hungarian proletariat and poorer peasantry. Apart from military defeat at the front, the downfall of the revolution was accelerated by the vacillating influence of the social democracy upon the Hungarian working class....

We, in Hungary, did not have the benefit of a mature Communist Party, and I am safe in saying that at the time we could not have such a Party. We had no mature Communist Party that could cling to the helm of State at the most critical moments, in spite of the wavering of the working class, in spite of the passive, and at times even hostile, attitude of part of the working class. In Hungary influence was brought to bear upon the masses of the proletariat by the fusion between the class-conscious active and determined minority and the social democracy, which, together, led the masses to the conquest of power. On the other hand, in Russia there has been, and there is now, a Communist Party with years of fighting experience, whose influence in the critical moments of the Russian Revolution was enormous....

...What is it that enabled the Russian Party not only to gain a majority at the time of the October revolution, but to retain it throughout the vicissitudes of the revolution? The secret lies first of all in the close organization of the Party. No other party, bourgeois or proletarian, had such a carefully picked and strongly welded nucleus, or to use a favorite military metaphor of Comrade Bukharin, a uniform ideological general staff, as has the Russian Party.

...The influence of the Communist Party over the large working class masses, with the State under Communist control, is naturally exercised

---

86. The reference is to the execution of Maximilien Robespierre (1758–1794) in the month of Thermidor, according to the revolutionary calendar, marking the end of the French Revolutionary Terror.

not only by means of propaganda, but also by the authority of the State and of the administration.

* * *

...In Russia, with the help of the Communist Party, the Soviets became a real popular institution, an organ of proletarian democracy. In Hungary we could not achieve this because there was no Communist leadership. But how is it possible to achieve united action in such a large country with so many State organs, with so many labour organizations? How is it possible, in a country where there are single districts much larger than France, Germany and England together, to find a unified party leadership which could be felt even in the smallest village?

How is centralization at all possible in such a country as Russia? I would like to answer this question by a comparison. In Germany the social-democracy, having attained power, was practically dissolved as a party organization. The governmental organs influenced the social democracy much more than the latter influenced the government. The deciding factor in the social-democracy is the governmental social-democratic bureaucracy which originated from the old party bureaucracy. It is just the opposite in Russia. The Russian Party always saw to it that the leading elements of the Party should influence the Soviet organs, and not vice-versa. To bring this about something was required from the Communist Party which is still not understood by many persons otherwise well acquainted with the Russian movement. This is what I said yesterday to one of the comrades of our Party: Russia is not a Prussian sergeant, and we are not recruits. Moscow represents the best leadership of the world revolution. Those who do not understand the significance of centralized discipline as the experience of the Russian Revolution created it are not good recruits of Communism or of the Communist Party....

How can we explain this discipline? Of course, there is the story that old-time Bolsheviks were an organization of conspirators under the leadership of Comrade Lenin. I am sorry to say that I was not a party to such conspiracy, and do not know what sort of conspirators they were. I know, however, that these conspirators have become the best leaders of the masses. Why? Because during this conspiring period of the Russian Revolution a strict discipline was created and the members of the Party were trained in this discipline. Naturally, this discipline comes not only from the masses, but mainly from the leaders, and it requires therefore a great confidence in the leaders. This leadership is really the heart of the Russian Communist Party, the authoritative body of the whole Communist movement. Allow me to quote these few words from the Austrian poet Anzengruber:[87] —*"Thou shalt honour thy father and thy mother, but they must be worthy of it."* The leaders of the Russian Revolution have gained the confidence of the masses and of the Communist Party because they have been worthy of it.

...The activity of the Communist Party of Russia should be a subject of study for every leader and organizer of the Western parties so that they may make critical use of the Russian experience in the Western situation and prepare their parties for the conquest and maintenance of power. The application of this experience is not the least problem of the International Revolution.

I am far from being an adherent of the free will doctrine, but I believe that for a realization of the prospects of a world revolution, the subjective factor of a Communist Party is one of the most important. We cannot determine the objective factors, at most we can influence them through the Communist Party. Nevertheless, I believe that if we had had Communist parties like the Russian one in 1919 in every country, at the time of the demobilization crisis, we would have been able not only to seize power, but also to have held it. The importance of the Communist Party as a subjective factor remains the same even in this period of comparative apathy. The question before us is: Considering the prospects for a world revolution, how can we build up such Communist parties which, in Western circumstances, perhaps through different means, can gradually win over the majority of the proletariat, before the revolution and after the revolution? Is it possible to create such Communist parties? I believe so. I have been working within the Communist Party of Russia, and I can say that the masses of its membership do not stand on a higher intellectual level than the German proletariat. I might even say that the masses of the German proletariat stand higher in culture than those of the Russian Communist Party. Of course, behind the Russian proletariat are five long years of experience in revolution; it is this experience which has made possible the elastic policy of the Russian Party.

But such elasticity is possible in all parties. I believe that the main problem in building up such subjective factors of the world revolution is the creation of basic revolutionary cadres. I believe that if we are able

---

87. Ludwig Anzengruber (1839–1889) was a Viennese writer.

to form these cadres, these vanguard troops, we will be able to lead the Western proletariat to the conquest of power, and retain this power after we have gained it. That is why this is one of our chief tasks, and the lessons which the Russian Communist Party has given us from five years of experience in the Russian Revolution are most important.

3.4
Otto Rühle, "Moscow and Us," 1920[88]

In the article below, Otto Rühle argues that the essence of communism is not centralization, discipline, and political control, but attaining superior levels of productivity, education, technology, and economic growth. Nor is there one single path to reach this goal.

Moscow and Us

I.

The *first* International was the International of *awakening*.

It had called upon the proletariat of the world to wake up, to arise; it had to proclaim the great slogan of Socialism.

It had a *propagandistic* duty.

The *second* International was the International of *organization*.

Its role was to gather the masses that had awoken to class consciousness, to educate them, to prepare them for the Revolution.

It had an *organizational* duty.

The *third* International is the International of *Revolution*.

It has to set the masses on the march and stimulate their revolutionary activity; it has to carry out the World Revolution and establish the proletarian dictatorship.

It has a *revolutionary* duty.

---

88. Source: *Die Aktion*, vol. 10, no. 37/38 (September 18, 1920): 505–7. Translated by Julia Sergeeva-Albova.

The *fourth* International will be the International of *Communism.*
It has to put the new economy in place, organize the new society,
establish socialism. It has to abolish dictatorship, dissolve the state, build
a—finally free!—society without dominance.

Its duty will be to *fulfill the communist idea.*

II.

The Third International calls itself Communist. It wants to be more
than it can be. It is revolutionary, no more and no less. Thus, it stands on
the highest step so far on the hierarchy of Internationals, and fulfills the
highest duty that has to be fulfilled and is possible to fulfill today.

It can be called the *Russian* International. It emerged in Russia. It is
based in Russia. It is ruled by Russia. Its spirit is outright the spirit of the
Russian Revolution, of the Russian Communist Party.

And exactly for this reason it cannot be a Communist International.

What in Russia attracts the regard of the world—regards of horror
and of admiration—is *not* yet Communism.

It is a Revolution, it is a class struggle of the Proletariat against the
Bourgeoisie, carried out with unprecedented determination, heroism,
and consequences. It is a dictatorship.

Russia is still far, many miles far from Communism. Russia, the *first*
country that came to Revolution and carried it out, will be the last land
that reaches Communism.

No, no—the Third International is *not* a Communist International!

III.

The Bolsheviks came to power in Russia not so much by means of a
revolutionary struggle for the socialist idea, but much more by means of
a *pacifistic coup.*

They promised *peace* to people.

And *land*—private property—to peasants.

This way they led all people after them.

And the coup succeeded.

They *jumped over a whole era,* the period of capitalist development.
From feudalism, whose breakdown began after 1905 and was accelerated
and completed by the war, they switched to socialism in a fabulous som-
ersault. At least they imagined that a political takeover by socialists was
enough to achieve a socialist era.

They believed they could *constructively* complete what should slowly
grow and ripen as a product of *natural* development.

Revolution and socialism were for them primarily a political matter. How could these perfect Marxists ever forget that they are primarily an *economic* matter?

The most mature capitalist production, highly developed technology, the most educated workers, highest returns on production—to name a few—are *indispensable* preconditions of the socialist economy and therefore of socialism itself.

Where could one find these preconditions in Russia?

A rapid proliferation of world revolution could *supply what is missing*. The Bolsheviks have done everything to induce it. *But it has failed so far to materialize.*

So arose a *vacuum*.

Political socialism without an economic foundation. A theoretic design. Bureaucratic rule. An accumulation of paper decrees. Agitational slogans. And terrible disappointment.

Russian Communism hangs in the air. And it will remain there until World Revolution creates conditions for its realization in the advanced capitalist countries that are the most ready for socialism.

IV.

The cascading Revolution is surging forward. It is hurtling over Germany. Soon it will reach other countries.

In every country, it will encounter *different* economic relations. A *different* social structure. *Different* traditions. *Different* ideologies. In every country, the stage of the political development of the proletariat is *different; different* is its relation to the bourgeoisie, to the peasants; *different* is therefore its method of class struggle.

In every country, the Revolution will have its *own face*. It will create its *own forms* and develop its *own laws*.

Revolution, although it is evolving into an international phenomenon, is in the first place a unique development for *each* country, *each* people.

However valuable Russia's revolutionary experience can be to the proletariat of any country, however thankful that country may be for brotherly advice and neighborly help—the Revolution itself is that country's *own* affair; it must be independent in its struggles, free in its decisions, free from influence and hindrance in its evaluation and utilization of the revolutionary situation.

The *Russian* Revolution is not the *German,* is not the World Revolution!

V.

In Moscow the opinion is different.

There, they have a *standard blueprint of Revolution.*

Allegedly the Russian Revolution unfolded according to this blueprint. This blueprint supposedly guided the Bolsheviks' struggle.

Consequently, the Revolution in the rest of the world must follow this blueprint.

Consequently, the parties in the other countries must conduct their struggle according to this blueprint.

Nothing is easier and simpler than this.

We have a Revolution...we have a revolutionary party...what do we do?

We take the usual blueprint of Revolution (patented by Lenin) out of our pocket, apply it...hurray! It works! And bang! The Revolution is won!

And what does this wonderful standard blueprint look like?

"The revolution is a *party affair.* The dictatorship is a *party affair.* Socialism is a *party affair."*

And further:

"The party is *discipline.* The party is *iron discipline.* The party is *leadership.* The party is the *strictest centralism.* The party is *militarism.* The party is the *most strict, most iron, most absolute militarism."*

Concretely formulated, this blueprint means:

The leaders are above; the masses are below.

Above: Authority. Bureaucratism. Personality cult. Dictatorship of the leader. Violent domination.

Below: Slavish obedience. Subordination. Standing at attention. Never-ending bigwigism.

The KPD[89] central office to the nth degree.

VI.

It is impossible to implement the Ludendorff system[90] in Germany for the second time, be it even in Bolshevik guise.

The Russian method of Revolution and of socialism is *unacceptable* for Germany, for the German proletariat.

---

89. The German Communist Party.

90. General Erich Ludendorff (1865–1937) was a dominant political figure during World War I who helped impose wide-ranging state controls over the economy.

We dismiss it. Absolutely. Categorically.
It would be a *disaster.*
More than that, it would be a *crime.*
It would lead us to *decay.*
Therefore we *want—can—have the right* to have *nothing* in common with an International that assumes that the Russian method should be imposed, even forced onto the proletariat of the world.
We must preserve for ourselves full freedom and independence.
The German proletariat will make its *German* Revolution, like the *Russian* proletariat made the *Russian* Revolution.
It has come to the Revolution *later.*
It will have to struggle *harder.*
Because of that, it will reach Communism *earlier* and *more assuredly.*

3.5
Romain Rolland Responds to a Call to Join the Revolutionary Cause, February 2, 1922[91]

Below is an excerpt from Romain Rolland's second open letter to Henri Barbusse in response to the latter's passionate call for all intellectuals to join the communist cause, which he believed was being advanced by the Russian Revolution. In his first reply, Rolland had already expressed his concern about a lack of self-criticism among the Communists. He was even more uneasy about their unequivocal embrace of violence at the dawn of what he feared would be "an era of upheavals" and "an Iron Age."

Our common enemy, my dear Barbusse, is the oppressive violence that exists in human society today. But you are seeking to fight violence with violence. In my view (as I already mentioned and I am not going to repeat myself) this method can only lead to mutual destruction. If you act

---

91. Source: Romain Rolland, "Deuxième Lettre de Rolland à Barbusse," in *Textes politiques, sociaux et philosophiques choisis*, ed. Jean Albertini (Paris: Éditions Sociales, 1970), 209–16 (here: 212, 213–16).

against your enemies in the same fashion as your enemies, just as the Germans and French did during the war, the social war may end in some sort of a Treaty of Versailles, a paper victory. Even so, this result would be catastrophic for everyone. I may be wrong, but in any case I plan to fight with other weapons.

...the first one is an intrepid struggle of the mind, of all the combined forces of reason mobilized in order to monitor, control, and pass judgment on the actions of those in power (as our valiant friends of the *Union of Democratic Control*[92] are doing), but also in order to ridicule, castigate, and assail malfeasance, emulating the steely criticism and embittered irony of Voltaire[93] and the Encyclopedists[94] who did more for the downfall of the royalty than the handful of hotheads who took the Bastille.

But there is another weapon, much more powerful, though equally suitable to the weak and the strong; it has already proved its effectiveness in other lands. It is surprising that nobody ever talks about it in France: it was used among the Anglo-Saxons by thousands of *conscientious objectors*, by means of which Mahatma Gandhi is now undermining the British Empire's domination of India—it is Civil Disobedience, and I do not say Non-Resistance, since, make no mistake about it, this is resistance of the highest caliber. To refuse to consent and to go along with a criminal State—no act of greater heroism could be accomplished by a man of our times....

...Much preoccupied with collective forces (I know as well as anyone their strong magnetic appeal), perhaps you do not attach adequate importance to the individual conscience—the self-sufficient, thoroughly self-sufficient and independent conscience, the mover of the world!...How many generations of sacrifices—some dazzling, many more obscure—did it take to build the new Christian world upon the indestructible ruins of Rome! Can the Revolution whose goal is to build fraternal unity among working human beings have less importance and be expected to have fewer delays before it reaches its goal?...

...No, the attitude I propose to my companions is not one of detachment and renunciation. Quite the opposite, I say: "Never sleep! Never

---

92. The Union of Democratic Control was a left-leaning British pressure group formed in 1914.

93. Voltaire (1694–1778) was a brilliant French thinker and social critic.

94. The editors and authors who contributed in 1751–1772 to the world's first truly comprehensive encyclopedia.

compromise! Never yield before injustice and lies!...Dare! Sacrifice your-selves! And rest assured, your efforts will not be in vain. Your toil belongs to the centuries to come. Do not complain that you have not reached your goal. Rejoice partaking in the work that goes infinitely beyond your life. This is the way for the living to taste immortality."

* * *

I am now asking my fellow writers, especially those who claim to march in the vanguard of thought:

Do you think that the present duty of an artist, or a scholar, of an intellectual is to join, like joining the army of the right cause in 1914, the army of the Revolution in 1922? Or does it seem to you that the best way to serve the cause of humanity and even of the Revolution is to preserve the integrity of your free thought, even against the Revolution itself, if it fails to recognize the vital necessity of liberty! For if it fails to do so, it would no longer be a source of renewal. It would be nothing but a new form of the monster of a hundred faces: Reaction.

3.6
Emma Goldman Rejects Bolshevik Policies, 1922–1923[95]

Born in the Russian Empire, Emma Goldman (1869–1940) emi-grated to the United States in 1885. Jailed repeatedly for civil disobedience and incitement to violence, she was deported back to Russia in 1919, during the Red Scare. She emigrated again in 1921, after the bloody suppression of the Kronstadt Rebellion, which to her meant "the Russian Revolution was no more." The

---

95. Source: Emma Goldman, *My Further Disillusionment in Russia* (Garden City, NY: Doubleday, Page, & Company, 1924), 65, 66, 73–74, 75–77.

following passage is taken from My Further Disillusionment in Russia *(1924).*

In February 1921, the workers of several Petrograd factories went on strike. The winter was an exceptionally hard one, and the people of the capital suffered intensely from cold, hunger, and exhaustion. They asked an increase of their food rations, some fuel and clothing. The complaints of the strikers, ignored by the authorities, presently assumed a political character. Here and there was also voiced a demand for the Constituent Assembly and free trade. The attempted street demonstration of the strikers was suppressed, the Government having ordered out the military *kursanti.*[96]

* * *

When the Kronstadt sailors learned what was happening in Petrograd they expressed their solidarity with the strikers in their economic and revolutionary demands, but refused to support any call for the Constituent Assembly. On March 1st, the sailors organized a mass meeting in Kronstadt, which was attended also by the Chairman of the All-Russian Central Executive Committee, Kalinin[97] (the presiding officer of the Republic of Russia), the Commander of the Kronstadt Fortress, Kuzmin, and the Chairman of the Kronstadt Soviet, Vassiliev. The meeting, held with the knowledge of the Executive Committee of the Kronstadt Soviet, passed a resolution approved by the sailors, the garrison, and the citizens' meeting of 16,000 persons. Kalinin, Kuzmin, and Vassiliev spoke against the resolution, which later became the basis of the conflict between Kronstadt and the Government. It voiced the popular demand for Soviets elected by the free choice of the people.

* * *

On March 7th Trotsky began the bombardment of Kronstadt, and on the 17th the fortress and city were taken, after numerous assaults

---

96. Cadets.

97. Mikhail Kalinin (1875–1946), a long-term Bolshevik, was also a member of the Central Committee of the Communist Party.

involving terrific human sacrifice. Thus Kronstadt was "liquidated" and the "counterrevolutionary plot" quenched in blood. The "conquest" of the city was characterized by ruthless savagery, although not a single one of the Communists arrested by the Kronstadt sailors had been injured or killed by them. Even before the storming of the fortress the Bolsheviki summarily executed numerous soldiers of the Red Army whose revolutionary spirit and solidarity caused them to refuse to participate in the bloodbath.

* * *

Seventeen dreadful days, more dreadful than anything I had known in Russia. Agonizing days, because of my utter helplessness in the face of the terrible things enacted before my eyes. It was just at that time that I happened to visit a friend who had been a patient in a hospital for months. I found him much distressed. Many of those wounded in the attack on Kronstadt had been brought to the same hospital, mostly *kursanti*. I had opportunity to speak to one of them. His physical suffering, he said, was nothing as compared with his mental agony. Too late he had realized that he had been duped by the cry of "counter-revolution." There were no Tsarist generals in Kronstadt, no White Guardists—he found only his own comrades, sailors and soldiers who had heroically fought for the Revolution.

The rations of the ordinary patients in the hospitals were far from satisfactory, but the wounded *kursanti* received the best of everything, and a select committee of Communist members was assigned to look after their comfort. Some of the *kursanti*, among them the man I had spoken to, refused to accept the special privileges. "They want to pay us for murder," they said. Fearing that the whole institution would be influenced by these awakened victims, the management ordered them removed to a separate ward, the "Communist ward," as the patients called it.

Kronstadt broke the last thread that held me to the Bolsheviki. The wanton slaughter they had instigated spoke more eloquently against them than aught else. Whatever their pretences in the past, the Bolsheviki now proved themselves the most pernicious enemies of the Revolution. I could have nothing further to do with them.

3.7
"The Russian Problem," 1919[98]

The memorandum excerpted below was written by Harald Scavenius (1873–1939), Danish ambassador to Russia. Scavenius worked hard to protect Russian noblemen from the Red Terror, but had to leave Russia once diplomatic relations were severed in December 1918. He then served as Denmark's foreign minister from 1920 to 1922. He presented his memorandum at the Paris Peace Conference in 1919, where leaders of Britain, France, the United States, and Italy worked to establish the principles of a post–World War I order. Scavenius was deeply disturbed by the connections between Soviet Russia and the revolutionary movement in Germany and made a case for a speedy destruction of Bolshevism.

One of the most important questions which is to be dealt with by the forthcoming Peace Conference will no doubt be the adjustment of the Russian chaos. On that point everybody agrees: disagreement only exists in regard to the question as to how this adjustment is to be brought about. For the sake of greater clearness the diverging opinions can be grouped under two main headings: Intervention or Non-Intervention.

* * *

A Bolshevist Germany will instantly ally itself with Russia and after this it will hardly be possible for the peace congress to enforce its decisions. In this respect the Brest-Litovsk peace is an object lesson. In order to avoid this and especially to guarantee a lasting peace it is necessary to finish off Bolshevism before it is too late. It is still feasible with comparatively small difficulties while it will prove rather impossible if action is postponed till also Germany has become Bolshevist at any rate not without the resumption of a new regular war which will perhaps prove to be more than can possibly be inflicted upon armies which after four and a half years of war have already been within the reach of peace.

---

98. Source: Harald Scavenius, "The Russian Problem" (1919), Papers of Richard Pipes, 1945–2006, HUG(FP)98.25, Box 4 of 7, Folder J, Harvard University Archives.

In the case that an intervention is decided upon one ought to avoid mistakes similar to those committed by Germany in occupying the Baltic provinces and Ukraine and leaving Petrograd and Moscow alone. It ought to be realized that if Bolshevism is going to be suppressed, it will be necessary to oust the Bolshevists from the said cities. As long as the Bolshevists are in possession of the Government machine and, masquerading as a Government, are able to continue their propaganda nothing will be gained by occupying ever so many provinces. No large forces are needed for the occupation of Moscow and Petrograd because the population of these cities are solidly opposed to the Bolshevists and a large percentage of the garrisons in these cities are likewise not real Bolshevists but ordinary citizens who by fear and distress have been compelled to join the red army. Part of the necessary troops may without doubt easily be enlisted among the soldiers now returning, many of which are more or less out of touch with civil life, nor will it prove difficult to enlist volunteers in Scandinavia. The troops collected in this way need not be very numerous because the greater part of the troops requisite for the occupation may be available through an agreement with the Finnish Government, and it will also be possible to organize the Russian troops in Finland. The offensive for Petrograd must of course be launched from Finland, the frontier of which is only 20 kilometers distant from the said city.

If intervention is decided upon the intervening countries ought instantly, i.e. pending discussions of details, to forward some cargoes of foodstuffs to Helsingfors in order to have the necessary stores ready in time for supplying the population of Petrograd and Moscow till foodstuffs can arrive from Siberia. During the present conditions while the population of the said cities is dying from starvation one wagon load of flour is worth more than many guns.

3.8

Adolf Hitler's Lessons from the Russian Revolution, 1923–1926[99]

Adolf Hitler began working on his main doctrinal book Mein Kampf *(My Struggle) while imprisoned for the failed Nazi coup attempt in Munich in 1923. It is debatable to what extent a book written in the mid-1920s can be used to explain Hitler's policy agenda after seizing power in 1933. But it sheds light on key premises of Hitler's worldview and his profound fear and hostility towards Bolshevism.*

* * *

Slowly fear of the Marxist weapon of Jewry descends like a nightmare on the mind and soul of decent people.

* * *

And in politics he [the Jew] begins to replace the idea of democracy by the dictatorship of the proletariat.

In the organized mass of Marxism he has found the weapon which lets him dispense with democracy and in its stead allows him to subjugate and govern the peoples with a dictatorial and brutal fist.

He works systematically for revolutionization in a twofold sense: economic and political.

Around peoples who offer too violent a resistance to attack from within he weaves a net of enemies, thanks to his international influence, incites them to war, and finally, if necessary, plants the flag of revolution on the very battlefields.

* * *

---

99. Source: Adolf Hitler, *Mein Kampf*, trans. Ralph Manheim (Boston and New York: Houghton Mifflin, 2001), 324, 325, 472, 475, 477, 524, 533, 649, 654–55, 662.

The most frightful example of this kind is offered by Russia, where he killed or starved about thirty million people with positively fanatical savagery, in part amid inhuman tortures, in order to give a gang of Jewish journalists and stock exchange bandits domination over a great people.[100]

* * *

What gave *Marxism* its astonishing power over the great masses is by no means the formal written work of the Jewish intellectual world, but rather the enormous oratorical propaganda wave which took possession of the great masses in the course of the years.

* * *

Let no one believe that the French Revolution would ever have come about through philosophical theories if it had not found an army of agitators led by demagogues in the grand style, who whipped up the passions of the people tormented to begin with, until at last there occurred that terrible volcanic eruption which held all Europe rigid with fear. And likewise the greatest revolutionary upheaval of the most recent period, the Bolshevist Revolution in Russia, was brought about, not by Lenin's writings, but by the hate-fomenting oratorical activity of countless of the greatest and the smallest apostles of agitation.

The illiterate common people were not, forsooth, fired with enthusiasm for the Communist Revolution by the theoretical reading of Karl Marx, but solely by the glittering heaven which thousands of agitators, themselves, to be sure, all in the service of an idea, talked into the people.

And that has always been so and will eternally remain so.

* * *

…For I must not measure the speech of a statesman to his people by the impression which it leaves in a university professor, but by the effect it exerts on the people. And this alone gives the standard for the speaker's genius.

---

100. As often was the case, Hitler constructed his own version of reality not based on facts. The total number of unnatural deaths from 1914 until 1922 was somewhat over ten million, including those due to World War I and the famine of 1921–1922. It was also absurd to suggest that any non-Bolshevik journalists, not to mention stockbrokers, gained from the Bolshevik regime.

* * *

Once it was possible in Russia to incite the uneducated hordes of the great masses, unable to read or write, against the thin intellectual upper crust that stood in no relation or connection to them, the fate of the country was decided, the revolution had succeeded; the Russian illiterate had thus become the defenseless slave of his Jewish dictators,[101] who for their part, it must be admitted, were clever enough to let this dictatorship ride on the phrase, of "people's dictatorship."

* * *

… *The lack of a great, creative, renewing idea means at all times a limitation of fighting force. Firm belief in the right to apply even the most brutal weapons is always bound up with the existence of a fanatical faith in the necessity of the victory of a revolutionary new order on this earth.*

A movement that is not fighting for such highest aims and ideals will, therefore, never seize upon the ultimate weapon.

The fact of having a new great idea to show was the secret of the success of the French Revolution; the Russian Revolution owes its victory to the idea, and only through the idea did fascism achieve the power to subject a people in the most beneficial way to the most comprehensive creative renewal.

Of this, bourgeois parties are not capable.

* * *

The demand for restoration of the frontiers of 1914 is a political absurdity of such proportions and consequences as to make it seem a crime. Quite aside from the fact that the Reich's frontiers in 1914 were anything but logical. For in reality they were neither complete in the sense of embracing the people of German nationality, nor sensible with regard to geo-military expediency. They were not the result of a considered political action, but momentary frontiers in a political struggle that was by no means concluded; partly, in fact, they were the results of chance.

---

101. Although a substantial minority of the Bolshevik leadership had Jewish origins, this was also true for their socialist and liberal opponents. As shown in previous chapters, the Bolsheviks were for the most part internationalist, atheistic, and in general opposed to ethnic, national, and religious distinctions.

* * *

And so we National Socialists consciously draw a line beneath the foreign policy tendency of our pre-War period. We take up where we broke off six hundred years ago.[102] *We stop the endless German movement to the south and west, and turn our gaze toward the land in the east. At long last we break off the colonial and commercial policy of the pre-War period and shift to the soil policy of the future.*

If we speak of soil in Europe today, we can primarily have in mind only Russia and her vassal border states.

Here Fate itself seems desirous of giving us a sign. By handing Russia to Bolshevism, it robbed the Russian nation of that intelligentsia which previously brought about and guaranteed its existence as a state. For the organization of a Russian state formation was not the result of the political abilities of the Slavs in Russia, but only a wonderful example of the state-forming efficacity of the German element in an inferior race. Numerous mighty empires on earth have been created in this way. Lower nations led by Germanic organizers and overlords have more than once grown to be mighty state formations and have endured as long as the racial nucleus of the creative state race maintained itself. For centuries Russia drew nourishment from this Germanic nucleus of its upper leading strata. Today it can be regarded as almost totally exterminated and extinguished. It has been replaced by the Jew. Impossible as it is for the Russian by himself to shake off the yoke of the Jew by his own resources, it is equally impossible for the Jew to maintain the mighty empire forever. He himself is no element of organization, but a ferment of decomposition. The Persian empire in the east is ripe for collapse. And the end of Jewish rule in Russia will also be the end of Russia as a state. We have been chosen by Fate as witnesses of a catastrophe which will be the mightiest confirmation of the soundness of the folkish[103] theory.

Our task, the mission of the National Socialist movement, is to bring our own people to such political insight that they will not see their goal for the future in the breath-taking sensation of a new Alexander's conquest, but in the industrious work of the German plow, to which the sword need only give soil.

---

102. Hitler was referring to the *Ostsiedlung*, the Germanic expansion into eastern Europe during the Middle Ages.

103. That is, German nationalist.

* * *

Germany is today the next great war aim of Bolshevism. It requires all the force of a young missionary idea to raise our people up again, to free them from the snares of this international serpent, and to stop the inner contamination of our blood, in order that the forces of the nation thus set free can be thrown in to safeguard our nationality, and thus can prevent a repetition of the recent catastrophes down to the most distant future. If we pursue this aim, it is sheer lunacy to ally ourselves with a power whose master is the mortal enemy of our future. How can we expect to free our own people from the fetters of this poisonous embrace if we walk right into it? How shall we explain Bolshevism to the German worker as an accursed crime against humanity if we ally ourselves with the organizations of this spawn of hell, thus recognizing it in the larger sense? By what right shall we condemn a member of the broad masses for his sympathy with an outlook if the very leaders of the state choose the representatives of this outlook for allies?

The fight against Jewish world Bolshevization requires a clear attitude toward Soviet Russia. You cannot drive out the Devil with Beelzebub.[104]

* * *

3.9
"The Zinoviev Letter" Roils British Politics, 1924[105]

The forged letter below was published by the Daily Mail *on October 25, 1924, days before new British national elections and became a major embarrassment to the Labor government. In 1999, a British government-affiliated scholar with access to secret service archives confirmed that the letter was leaked to the*

---

104. Here, Hitler, in a metaphor he returned to throughout his career, was paraphrasing Jesus, as related in Matt. 12:26–27.

105. Source: Gill Bennett, *A Most Extraordinary and Mysterious Business: The Zinoviev Letter of 1924* (London: Foreign & Commonwealth Office, General Services Command, 1999), 93–95.

press by MI6 operatives. Who exactly forged the Russian original, which contains spelling, grammar, and syntactic errors, remains a mystery.

SOVIET RUSSIA   Latvia
                                        L/3900
                                        2.10.24
                                        Instructions to British Communist Party

VERY SECRET   Executive Committee, Third
                                        Communist International.
                                        Presidium.
                                        Sept 15th, 1924.

To the Central Committee,
    British Communist Party.
    Moscow.

Dear Comrades,

The time is approaching for the Parliament of England to consider the Treaty concluded between the Governments of Great Britain and the S.S.S.R. for the purpose of ratification. The fierce campaign raised by the British bourgeoisie around the question shows that the majority of the same, together with reactionary circles, are against the Treaty for the purpose of breaking off an agreement consolidating the ties between the proletariats of the two countries leading to the restoration of normal relations between England and the S.S.S.R.

The proletariat of Great Britain, which pronounced its weighty word when danger threatened a break-off of the past negotiations, and compelled the Government of MacDonald to conclude the Treaty, must show the greatest possible energy in the further struggle for ratification and against the endeavours of British capitalists to compel Parliament to annul it.

It is indispensable to stir up the masses of the British proletariat, to bring into movement the army of unemployed proletarians, whose position can be improved only after a loan has been granted to the S.S.S.R. for the restoration of her economies and when business collaboration between the British and Russian proletariats has been put in order. It is imperative that the group in the Labour Party sympathising with the Treaty should bring increased pressure to bear upon the Government and parliamentary circles in favour of the ratification of the Treaty.

Keep close observation over the leaders of the Labour Party, because those may easily be found in the leading strings of the bourgeoisie. The foreign policy of the Labour Party as it is already represents an inferior copy of the policy of the Curzon Government.[106] Organise a campaign of disclosures of the foreign policy of MacDonald.

The IKKI[107] will willingly place at your disposal the wide material in its possession regarding the activities of British imperialism in the Middle and Far East. In the meanwhile, however, strain every nerve in the struggle for the ratification of the treaty, in favour of a continuation of negotiations regarding the regulation of relations between the S.S.S.R. and England. A settlement of relations between the two countries will assist in the revolutionising of the international and British proletariat not less than a successful rising in any of the working districts of England, as the establishment of close contact between the British and Russian proletariat, the exchange of delegations and workers, etc., will make it possible for us to extend and develop the propaganda of ideas of Leninism in England and the Colonies. Armed warfare must be preceded by a struggle against the inclinations to compromise which are embedded among the majority of British workmen, against the ideas of evolution and peaceful extermination of capitalism. Only then will it be possible to count upon complete success of an armed insurrection. In Ireland and the Colonies the case is different; there, there is a national question, and this represents too great a factor for success for us to waste time on a prolonged preparation of the working class.

But even in England, as in other countries where the workers are politically developed, events themselves may more rapidly revolutionise the working masses than propaganda. For instance, a strike movement, repressions by the Government, etc.

From your last report it is evident that agitation-propaganda work in the Army is weak, in the Navy a very little better. Your explanation that the quality of the members attracted justifies the quantity is right in principle, nevertheless it would be desirable to have cells in all the units of

---

106. Lord Curzon (1859–1925) was a conservative statesman who served as Secretary of State for Foreign Affairs from 1919 to 1924 but was never head of government.

107. The Comintern.

the troops, particularly among those quartered in the large centres of the country, and also among factories working on munitions and at military store depots. We request that the most particular attention be paid to these latter.

In the event of danger of war, with the aid of the latter and in contact with the transport workers, it is possible to paralyse all the military preparations of the bourgeoisie and to make a start in turning an imperialist war into a class war. Now more than ever we should be on our guard. Attempts at intervention in China show that world imperialism is still full of vigour and is once more making endeavours to restore its shaken position and cause a new war, which as its final objective is to bring about the break-up of the Russian proletariat and the suppression of the budding world revolution, and further would lead to the enslavement of the colonial peoples. "Danger of War," "The Bourgeoisie seeks War; Capital fresh Markets."—these are the slogans which you must familiarise the masses with, with which you must go to work into the mass of the proletariat. Those slogans will open to you the doors of comprehension of the masses, will help you to capture them and march under the banner of Communism.

The Military Section of the British Communist Party, so far as we are aware, further suffers from a lack of specialists, the future directors of the British Red Army.

It is time you thought of forming such a group, which, together with the leaders, might be, in the event of an outbreak of active strife, the brain of the military organisation of the Party.

Go attentively through the lists of the military "cells," detailing from them the more energetic and capable men, turn attention to the more talented military specialists who have, for one reason or another, left the Service and hold socialist views. Attract them into the ranks of the Communist Party if they desire honestly to serve the proletariat and desire in the future to direct not the blind mechanical forces in the service of the bourgeoisie, but a national army.

Form a directing operative head of the Military Section.

Do not put this off to a future moment, which may be pregnant with events and catch you unprepared.

Desiring you all success, both in organisation and in your struggle,

With Communist Greetings,

President of the Presidium of the IKKI

ZINOVIEV
Member of the Presidium
McManus.
Secretary, KUUSINEN
Copies to
London
Estonia
Finland
Legation
File

3.10
Neville Chamberlain's Unease about Soviet Russia, 1939[108]

From 1915 to his death in 1940, Neville Chamberlain regularly corresponded with his sisters, Ida and Hilda. The format of private letters allowed him to share his thoughts and calculations on political and diplomatic matters that could not be made public at the time. In the excerpted letter below, Chamberlain explains his and other European politicians' distrust of Soviet Russia, which stood in the way of forging a robust anti-Hitler coalition in 1939.

26 March 1939

Chequers

My dear Ida,
From your letter I think you have realized that this has been a grim week though how grim even you couldn't know.

* * *

───────────

108. Source: Robert Self, ed. *The Neville Chamberlain Diary Letters*, 4 vols. (London: Ashgate, 2005), 4:396.

The only line of advance that presented itself to me after the Czecho-Slovakian affair was to get a declaration signed by the four Powers: Britain, France, Russia & Poland that they would act together in the event of further signs of German aggressive ambitions. I drafted the formula myself and sent it out. But it soon became evident that Poland would find great difficulty in signing and I could really understand why. Hitherto she has skillfully balanced between Germany & Russia so as to not get into trouble with either. But if she now joins with Russia & the Western democracies in a declaration which aims at curbing German ambitions, will not the Germans say to her, Aha! Now we see where you stand. Unless you instantly abjure your new friends, hand over Dantzig [*sic*] and accept whatever humiliating conditions we impose we will bomb Warsaw into ruins in a few hours. And what consolation would it be to know that *thereafter* Britain & France would make Germany pay for her behavior; it's like sending a man into the lions den and saying to him: "Never mind if the lion does gobble you up; I intend to give him a good hiding afterwards." As soon as I appreciated this position fully I saw that it was unlikely that we should get their signature. Was it worth while to go on with Russia in that case? I must confess to the most profound distrust of Russia. I have no belief whatever in her ability to maintain an effective offensive even if she wanted to. And I distrust her motives which seem to me to have little connection with our ideas of liberty and to be concerned only with getting everyone else by the ears. Moreover, she is both hated and suspected by many of the smaller states notably by Poland, Rumania, and Finland so that our close association with her might easily cost us the sympathy of those who would much more effectively help us if we can get them on our side.

My conclusion therefore is that the Declaration is dead...

3.11

"A Bright and a Heartening Phenomenon in a Dark and Dismal World," 1933–1936[109]

In the following excerpt, taken from his autobiography, Jawaharlal Nehru recalls the period after 1933, when two attempts of his National Congress Party to hold sessions in Delhi and Calcutta were forcibly dispersed by the police. Champions of Indian independence found few venues for legal political work and in response embraced campaigns of civil disobedience in which Mohandas Gandhi (1869–1948) took the lead. Prospects for quick success looked dim and morale was fading. Nehru describes how he came to be drawn to Marxism and how the example of Soviet Russia sustained him through these hard times.

As our struggle toned down and stabilized itself at a low level, there was little of excitement in it, except at long intervals. My thoughts traveled more to other countries, and I watched and studied, as far as I could in gaol, the world situation in the grip of the great depression. I read as many books as I could find on the subject, and the more I read the more fascinated I grew. India with her problems and struggles became just a part of this mighty world drama, of the great struggle of political and economic forces that was going on everywhere, nationally and internationally. In that struggle my own sympathies went increasingly toward the communist side.

I had long been drawn to socialism and communism, and Russia had appealed to me. Much in Soviet Russia I dislike—the ruthless suppression of all contrary opinion, the wholesale regimentation, the unnecessary violence (as I thought) in carrying out various policies. But there was no lack of violence and suppression in the capitalist world, and I realized more and more how the very basis and foundation of our acquisitive society and property was violence. Without violence it could not continue for many days. A measure of political liberty meant little indeed when the fear of starvation was always compelling the vast majority of

---

109. Source: Jawaharlal Nehru, *An Autobiography with Musings on Recent Events in India* (London: John Lane, 1936), 361–63.

people everywhere to submit to the will of the few, to the greater glory and advantage of the latter.

Violence was common in both places, but the violence of the capitalist order seemed inherent in it; while the violence of Russia, bad though it was, aimed at a new order based on peace and cooperation and real freedom for the masses. With all her blunders, Soviet Russia had triumphed over enormous difficulties and taken great strides toward this new order. While the rest of the world was in the grip of the Depression and going backward in some ways, in the Soviet country a great new world was being built up before our eyes. Russia, following the great Lenin, looked into the future and thought only of what was to be, while other countries lay numbed under the dead hand of the past and spent their energy in preserving the useless relics of a bygone age. In particular, I was impressed by the reports of the great progress made by the backward regions of Central Asia under the Soviet regime. In the balance, therefore, I was all in favor of Russia, and the presence and example of the Soviets was a bright and heartening phenomenon in a dark and dismal world.

But Soviet Russia's success or failure, vastly important as it was as a practical experiment in establishing a communist state, did not affect the soundness of the theory of communism. The Bolsheviks may blunder or even fail because of national or international reasons, and yet the communist theory may be correct. On the basis of that very theory it was absurd to copy blindly what had taken place in Russia, for its application depended on the particular conditions prevailing in the country in question and the stage of its historical development. Besides, India, or any other country, could profit by the triumphs as well as the inevitable mistakes of the Bolsheviks. Perhaps the Bolsheviks had tried to go too fast because, surrounded as they were by a world of enemies, they feared external aggression. A slower tempo might avoid much of the misery caused in the rural areas.[110] But then the question arose if really radical results could be obtained by slowing down the rate of change. Reformism was an impossible solution of any vital problem at a critical moment when the basic structure had to be changed, and however slow the progress might be later on, the initial step must be a complete break with the existing order, which had fulfilled its purpose and was now only a drag on future progress.

---

110. This may have been a reference to the collectivization of agriculture from 1929 and the terrible famine of 1932–1933.

In India, only a revolutionary plan could solve the two related questions of the land and industry as well as almost every other major problem before the country....

Russia apart, the theory and philosophy of Marxism lightened up many a dark corner of my mind. History came to have a new meaning for me. The Marxist interpretation threw a flood of light on it, and it became an unfolding drama with some order and purpose, howsoever unconscious, behind it. In spite of the appalling waste and misery of the past and the present, the future was bright with hope, though many dangers intervened. It was the essential freedom from dogma and the scientific outlook of Marxism that appealed to me. It was true that there was plenty of dogma in official communism in Russia and elsewhere, and frequently heresy hunts were organized. That seemed to be deplorable, though it was not difficult to understand in view of the tremendous changes taking place rapidly in the Soviet countries when effective opposition might have resulted in catastrophic failure.

The great world crisis and slump seemed to justify the Marxist analysis. While all other systems and theories were groping about in the dark, Marxism alone explained it more or less satisfactorily and offered a real solution.

As this conviction grew upon me, I was filled with a new excitement, and my depression at the nonsuccess of civil disobedience grew much less. Was not the world marching rapidly toward the desired consummation? There were grave dangers of wars and catastrophes, but at any rate we were moving. There was no stagnation. Our national struggle became a stage in the longer journey, and it was as well that repression and suffering were tempering our people for future struggles and forcing them to consider the new ideas that were stirring the world. We would be the stronger and the more disciplined and hardened by the elimination of the weaker elements. Time was in our favor.

3.12
Josiah Gumede, "The New Jerusalem," 1927[111]

Josiah Tshangana Gumede (1867–1946) was a leading South African radical activist. He visited the Soviet Union in November–December 1927 during an official celebration of the tenth anniversary of the October Revolution. Under the headline "Gumede Brings Keys to Freedom," the official newspaper of the Communist Party of South Africa, the South African Worker, *reported on the message he brought back to Africa.*

RECEPTION TO J.T. GUMEDE AT PARTY HEADQUARTERS

The Communist Hall at Johannesburg was crowded to suffocation last Saturday night to welcome J.T. Gumede, Pres. Gen. of the African National Congress, on his return from Russia, where he had attended the Tenth Anniversary Celebration and the "Friends of Russia" convention in November, subsequently touring several of the Eastern and Southern Soviet Republics united in the U.S.S.R.

* * *

NEW HOPE OF OPPRESSED PEOPLES

He recalled the failure of his previous visits to Imperialist England, the new hope inspired at the Brussels Conference[112] a year ago, and finally the solid support for the cause of all oppressed peoples which he had met with at Moscow. There he found that all he had been told of Russia

---

111. Source: "To Destroy Oppression and Smash Class Rule," *South African Worker*, vol. 12 (March 2, 1928): 1; "African National Congress Welcomes Gumede," ibid., 2.

112. The 1927 Brussels Conference was convened under the auspices of the League against Imperialism, a front organization of the Comintern.

was lies. Instead of exploiters and exploited, tyrants and downtrodden, he found everyone a friend and comrade: education for all, even for old women, and no one said "this is mine," but "this is ours." Even the prisoners had a freedom unknown to many "freemen" in Africa, with weekend leave to visit their homes, orchestras and theaters of their own, weekly newspapers edited by themselves and circulating in all the prisons of the country, and, for disciplinary offenses, an arbitration court consisting of fellow prisoners. The country was owned by its people, and the Government supplied agricultural implements and financed their cooperative stores. The sailors at sea and ashore had as comfortable a time as the rest. In short, "Jim" was the ruler of the country.

This wonderful liberation had been accomplished by organising and fighting with weapons torn from the oppressors. And throughout, he found that the people who were able to reason and to lead the class struggle were the Communists. (Cheers.)

* * *

A NEW JERUSALEM

* * *

"I am one of the blessed sons of your mothers for I have seen the new world to come, where it has actually begun. I have been to the new Jerusalem."

For centuries the Russian people suffered under the tyranny and despotism of the Tsarist Empire, which subjected and oppressed many countries under a terrible burden of suffering and exploitation.

Imperialism cut the land into farms leaving the people landless; the people had to work for nobles for little or no pay, reduced to dire poverty, weeping, and wailing, always being raided, shot by police; this made them unite and finally they kicked out the oppressors, killed the Tsar, and took the land and towns for the people.

* * *

NATIONAL INDEPENDENCE FOR ALL RACES

I have brought back a key with me if you will accept it; we need your help and support to turn that key and unlock the door to freedom....

3.13

W. E. B. Du Bois Discovers Soviet Russia (c. 1928)[113]

The article excerpted below focuses on one aspect of the Russian Revolution that W. E. B. Du Bois thought to be crucial for Black Americans—its emphasis on racial equality. The article was written around 1928, after his journey to the USSR.

Whatever we may think theoretically of Russia's revolution and the Soviet government two things are certainly true—first, the economic system based on private capital which is prevalent in the world today is imperfect and is and has been widely criticized. There is scarcely a student of the system past and present who does not regard it as a makeshift which can and must be improved. Whether the dictatorship of the proletariat as exemplified in Russia will bring the needed improvements or not, only time will tell. But certainly this second proposition cannot be controverted: we must judge Russia by what she does and not simply by what she says and certainly not by what other people say about her. We must remember that private interests both economic and social wish the failure of the Russian experiment and we must listen to their voices in books, speeches, and the public press with reserve.

To us as Negro Americans, the chief question is: What is Russia's attitude toward the world problem of race? We include in this, her attitude toward Negroes in America and Africa and toward the colored peoples of the East. This is not all. Most Americans do not know that within Russia are numerous race problems. The territory of the union of the Soviet republics consists of over eight million square miles, or one-sixth of the

113. Source: Du Bois, W. E. B. (William Edward Burghardt), 1868–1963. Russia and the race problem, c. 1928. W. E. B. Du Bois Papers (MS 312). Special Collections and University Archives, University of Massachusetts Amherst Libraries.

land surface of the earth and of one hundred and fifty million people of different races and languages, including five varieties of Slavs, two sets of Lithuanians, five of the Latin and Teutonic races, seven Iranians, ten varieties of Finns, twelve groups of Turks and Tartars, two sets of Monguls, besides Jews, Gypsies, Chinese, Japanese, Koreans, and five or six other races. No such tremendous mixture of race under one government has been seen elsewhere in the world, not even in the United States of America.

Here then, above all, is the place to ask: How does the new revolutionary government of Russia face the question of race? And the answer is clear and unequivocal. Russia stands for absolute equality of races—political, social, and civil. She recognizes on the one hand the rights of her constituent peoples to maintain their own language and their own culture and to have schools, teachers, and literature to sustain these. So far as practicable, she gives all the different nations local governmental autonomy. Russia consists of ten autonomous soviet socialistic republics; and within these republics, are various partially autonomous governments based on race and language.

On the other hand, Russia does not force racial segregation. A Tartar may send his child to a Tartar school or to a Russian school, just as he pleases. In the Tartar school, he learns Russian. Every inducement is held out to make the different groups acquainted with the language and the culture of the leading races in Russia. But they are not forced to this. They are invited.

* * *

What will be the result of this experiment in the encouragement of races and nations, groups and languages, within a great nation? Usually nations have tried to suppress variant groups. They have hammered and pounded them into submission and disappearance as the Germans sought to do with the Poles, as the Hungarians treated the Slavs, and as England, France, and Spain have treated numerous smaller groups. Here in America, we are trying to make Germans, Irish, Hungarians, and Italians ashamed of the race that gave them birth, unwilling to remember their languages and claiming only English descent. Russia has set her face in the opposite direction. For the first time in decades, the Ukraine can be proud of its literature and language; the Poles can talk Polish, the Armenians can have their own little government, the Jews can not only be free in their own Soviet republic, but everywhere they wish to go in Russia.

That is not all. The colored peoples of the East—the dark Tartars, the Chinese, and the Monguls within the bounds of the Russian republic,—are given every encouragement. In Moscow there is a university for the Eastern peoples with a thousand students, with everything—clothes, food, and tuition—free. There is a Chinese university with about five hundred students giving a course of two years.

And finally in all public celebrations, the importance of the different racial elements in Russia is given free and frank encouragement. I saw the tenth annual celebration of Youth Day in September 1926. Two hundred thousand children and youth marched in the public square. They were not only Russians of all sorts and kinds but over one hundred Chinese and many Tartars, Caucasians, and people from Turkestan and two or three Negroes. I have never seen a greater variety of human types.

Not only in Russia, but outside of Russia and in her general diplomacy and relations in the world, Russia has taken a firm stand for racial equality. She has demanded decent treatment for Africans and persons of African descent throughout the world and has gone out of her way to treat Negro visitors with courtesy.

Above all, today Russia is the hope of Asia. She is the backbone of the present Chinese revolution and the hope of nationalism in India. This is the reason and the sole reason for the recent attack upon Russia in England, America, and Italy and to some extent in France. The solidarity of white Europe toward the colored world has been broken by Russia and the white world, led by England, is determined to punish Russia at any cost.

All this is quite outside of questions of economic policy, of political trend, and of debt settlements. The attitude of Russia on the race question within and without her boundaries is of tremendous significance to us and of such significance to the races of the world that it bids fair to overshadow other and in many respects lesser questions.

3.14
José Carlos Mariátegui Welcomes World Revolution[114]

The excerpt below is taken from a lecture given by José Carlos Mariátegui on September 28, 1923, in Lima, Peru, soon after his return from Europe where he observed the expanding repercussions of the Russian Revolution and met with leading revolutionaries and intellectuals, including Antonio Gramsci, Georges Sorel, Henri Barbusse, and Romain Rolland. Mariátegui praises the Comintern for recognizing that the world revolution is impossible without engaging the oppressed masses of Asia.

Only European and American workers were represented in the First International. The most advanced South American workers and workers drawn into the orbit of the European world, the western world, also took part in the Second International. But the Second International was still primarily an association of workers in the West, an appendage of European civilization and society. All this was natural and just, moreover, because the socialist doctrine, the proletarian doctrine, constituted a creation, a product of European and Western civilization. I said, to expound rapidly on the crisis of democracy, the socialist and proletarian doctrine is the child of bourgeois capitalist society.... Among the Eastern peoples, the system of slavery persists to this day. The problems of the peoples of the East are different from those of the peoples of the West....

The socialists have begun to understand that social revolution must not be only a European revolution, but a worldwide revolution. The leaders of the social revolution perceive and understand the capitalist tactic of seeking in the colonies resources and means of avoiding or delaying revolution in Europe. And they strive to fight capitalism, not only in Europe, not only in the West, but in the colonies. The Third International is driving socialist tactics in this new direction. The Third International encourages and promotes insurrection among the peoples of the East,

---

114. Source: José Carlos Mariátegui, "La agitatión revolucionaria y socialista del mundo oriental," in *Historia de la Crisis Mundial: Conferencias (Años 1923 y 1924)*, 7th ed. (Lima: Biblioteca Amauta, 1980), 140–47 [here: 142–46].

even though such popular actions lack a proletarian and class character, and exhibit, rather, a nationalist character.

* * *

At a memorable congress, the Congress of Halle,[115] Zinoviev, in the name of the Third International, defended its colonial policy against attacks by Hilferding,[116] the socialist leader and current Minister of Finance. On this occasion, Zinoviev was arguing, "The Second International was limited to white men; the Third does not divide men by the color of their skin. If you want a world revolution, if you want to liberate the proletariat from the chains of capitalism, you must not think only of Europe. You ought to also direct your gaze to Asia. Hilferding will reply scornfully: 'These Asians, these Tartars, these Chinese!' Comrades, I say a world revolution is not possible if we do not turn our faces also to Asia. Those lands are inhabited by four times more men than in Europe, and these men are as oppressed and outraged as we are.

"Are we going to move toward socialism or not? If Marx asserted that a European revolution without England would resemble no more than a tempest in a glass of water, we will say, oh comrades from Germany, that a proletarian revolution without Asia is not a world revolution. And this is very important for us. I am also European like you; but I feel that Europe is a small part of the world. At the Congress in Moscow,[117] we understood what so far has been lacking in the proletarian movement. We sensed what is necessary for the coming of the world revolution. And this something is the awakening of the oppressed masses of Asia. I confess: when in Baku we saw hundreds of Persians and Turks singing the 'Internationale' with us,[118] I felt tears in my eyes. And then I heard the rumbling of the world revolution."

---

115. Meeting in Halle, Germany, in October 1920, the Congress of the USPD, the Independent Socialist Party of Germany, voted to join the Third International.

116. Rudolf Hilferding (1877–1941) was a Marxist economist and politician of the SPD, or German Socialist Party.

117. Zinoviev is referring to the Second World Congress of the Comintern, which met from July 19 to August 7, 1920.

118. The Congress of the Peoples of the East was a multinational conference organized by the Comintern and held in Baku, Azerbaijan, in September 1920.

And it is for such reasons that the Third International has not wanted to be an exclusively European International. At the founding Congress of the Third International,[119] delegates from the Chinese Workers' Party and the Korean Workers Union were present. At the following congresses, Persians, Turkestanis, Armenians, and delegates from other Eastern peoples also attended. And on August 14, 1920, in Baku there gathered this great congress of the peoples of the East, to which Zinoviev alluded and which was attended by delegates from 24 Eastern peoples. At this congress, the foundations were laid for an International of the East, not a Socialist International, but a revolutionary and insurrectional one.

3.15

Dr. José Lanauze Rolón's Radio Address in Puerto Rico Extolls the Russian Revolution, 1936[120, 121]

José Lanauze Rolón (1893–1951) was an Afro-Puerto Rican physician who received his medical degree from Howard University and then completed specialized training in otorhinolaryngology at the University of Paris-Sorbonne. In 1925, he founded the Puerto Rican League for Birth Control (LPCNPR) and led the movement to decriminalize the publication and distribution of contraceptive information. A highly educated and prolific poet, essayist, and journalist, Lanauze was also a founding member of the Communist Party of Puerto Rico (1934–1944), and a leading internationalist theoretician. His speech for the nineteenth anniversary celebration of the Bolshevik take-over, excerpted below, reflects his belief in the progressive role of the Russian Revolution

---

119. The Third International was founded in Moscow in March 1919.

120. Our special thanks to Christian Vélez, Ph.D. student and research assistant to Dr. Sandra Pujals, Department of History, University of Puerto Rico, Río Piedras, for identifying the source at the *Colección Puertorriqueña*.

121. Source: Except from the speech "La Revolución Rusa: 19 aniversario" by Dr. José A. Lanauze Rolón, transmitted by WKAQ radio station in San Juan, Puerto Rico, on November 7, 1936, and later published as a pamphlet by the Communist Party of Puerto Rico (Third International). The copy of the pamphlet is from *Colección Puertorriqueña*, Biblioteca José M. Lázaro, Universidad de Puerto Rico, Río Piedras.

and its global significance, including its legacy to the Spanish Republic, which was then in the midst of a civil conflict. The speech was broadcast via San Juan radio in 1936.

What is the balance sheet of the Russian Revolution over the past nineteen years? Nineteen years in the history of a people is not very much. What has Puerto Rico, as a people, accomplished in those nineteen years? What about the other peoples of the Americas? What progress has the rich and vibrant metropolis to the north made in the past nineteen years?

Let's look at the record, as President Roosevelt has said. Let's look at the record of the Russian Revolution. At the end of those nineteen years, of the confusion, prostration and anarchy, misery and social paralysis, deeply rooted ignorance and superstition, and ancient slavery of the peasantry all that remains in the Soviet Union are scanty and indistinct traces. Russia is now the second largest industrial nation in Europe. It has liquidated in this short time the plague of illiteracy. Eighty percent of its agriculture, which adheres to the latest methods of mechanization and scientific cultivation, has been collectivized. Soviet science and the arts have nothing to envy the rest of the civilized world. In Russia there is no unemployment, there is social security for all, and the factories, land, and other means of production are in the hands of the workers. In Soviet Russia, to exploit others and increase one's profits through the labor of others is a crime, the greatest of crimes. Education is compulsory and free. Women have the same political, social and economic opportunities as men; mothers enjoy significant privileges and protections. Russia is still, as on the first day of the Revolution, the mother country of the child; the child in Russia is honored by the government, the intellectuals, and the entire work force.

While performing these enormous tasks of construction, of organization, and of social and moral development, Soviet Russia has been painfully forced to build up and discipline a powerful military force: an army of millions of soldiers, an air force of thousands of mighty airplanes, impregnable fortifications, an extremely efficient war industry, submarines, and numerous battleships. All of this makes Russia one of the greatest military powers in the world—and all of these marvelous achievements have come to fruition in the short span of less than half a generation.

Those victories in science, the arts, industry, agriculture, the military, and social life alone would suffice to prove the clear advantages of socialism as compared to capitalism, which remains mired in misery and insoluble problems. Those victories alone would suffice to make Russia the guiding light and inspiration of all the working masses of all the countries of the planet.

3.16

Mao Zedong's Retrospective of the Revolutionary Struggle, 1949[122]

In the document below, which was written in the summer of 1949, Mao Zedong speaks optimistically and in a broad revolutionary context of the struggle and goals of the Communist Party of China. There were good reasons for his optimism: by that point the Communists' struggle with the Guomindang was nearing an end. The Guomindang government had already fled the capital city of Nanking and on October 1, 1949, the Communist People's Republic of China would be officially proclaimed in Beijing.

The first of July 1949 marks the fact that the Communist Party of China has already lived through twenty-eight years. Like a man, a political party has its childhood, youth, manhood and old age. The Communist Party of China is no longer a child or a lad in his teens but has become an adult. When a man reaches old age, he will die; the same is true of a party. When classes disappear, all instruments of class struggle—parties and the state machinery—will lose their function, cease to be necessary, therefore gradually wither away and end their historical mission; and human society will move to a higher stage. We are the opposite of the political parties of the bourgeoisie. They are afraid to speak of the extinction of classes, state power, and parties. We, on the contrary, declare openly that we are striving hard to create the very conditions which will

---

122. Source: *Selected Works of Mao Tse-tung*, 5 vols. (Peking: Foreign Languages Press, 1969), 4:411–14, 415, 422–23.

bring about their extinction. The leadership of the Communist Party and the state power of the people's dictatorship are such conditions. Anyone who does not recognize this truth is no Communist. Young comrades who have not studied Marxism-Leninism and have only recently joined the Party may not yet understand this truth. They must understand it— only then can they have a correct world outlook. They must understand that the road to the abolition of classes, to the abolition of state power and to the abolition of parties is the road all mankind must take; it is only a question of time and conditions. Communists the world over are wiser than the bourgeoisie, they understand the laws governing the existence and development of things, they understand dialectics, and they can see farther. The bourgeoisie does not welcome this truth because it does not want to be overthrown. To be overthrown is painful and is unbearable to contemplate for those overthrown, for example, for the Kuomintang reactionaries whom we are now overthrowing and for Japanese imperialism which we together with other peoples overthrew some time ago. But for the working class, the labouring people, and the Communist Party the question is not one of being overthrown, but of working hard to create the conditions in which classes, state power, and political parties will die out very naturally and mankind will enter the realm of Great Harmony.[123] We have mentioned in passing the long-range perspective of human progress in order to explain clearly the problems we are about to discuss.

As everyone knows, our Party passed through these twenty-eight years not in peace but amid hardships, for we had to fight enemies, both foreign and domestic, both inside and outside the Party. We thank Marx, Engels, Lenin, and Stalin for giving us a weapon. This weapon is not a machine-gun, but Marxism-Leninism.

In his book *"Left-Wing" Communism, an Infantile Disorder* written in 1920, Lenin described the quest of the Russians for revolutionary theory. Only after several decades of hardship and suffering did the Russians find Marxism. Many things in China were the same as, or similar to, those in Russia before the October Revolution. There was the same feudal oppression. There was similar economic and cultural backwardness. Both countries were backward, China even more so. In both countries

---

123. The expression refers to a society based on public ownership, free from class exploitation and oppression—a lofty ideal long cherished by the Chinese people. Here Mao means communist society.

alike, for the sake of national regeneration progressives braved hard and bitter struggles in their quest for revolutionary truth.

From the time of China's defeat in the Opium War of 1840, Chinese progressives went through untold hardships in their quest for truth from the Western countries....Chinese who then sought progress would read any book containing the new knowledge from the West. The number of students sent to Japan, Britain, the United States, France, and Germany was amazing. At home, the imperial examinations were abolished and modern schools sprang up like bamboo shoots after a spring rain; every effort was made to learn from the West. In my youth, I too engaged in such studies. They represented the culture of Western bourgeois democracy, including the social theories and natural sciences of that period, and they were called "the new learning" in contrast to Chinese feudal culture, which was called "the old learning." For quite a long time, those who had acquired the new learning felt confident that it would save China, and very few of them had any doubts on this score, as the adherents of the old learning had. Only modernization could save China, only learning from foreign countries could modernize China. Among the foreign countries, only the Western capitalist countries were then progressive, as they had successfully built modern bourgeois states. The Japanese had been successful in learning from the West, and the Chinese also wished to learn from the Japanese. The Chinese in those days regarded Russia as backward, and few wanted to learn from her. That was how the Chinese tried to learn from foreign countries in the period from the 1840s to the beginning of the 20th century.

Imperialist aggression shattered the fond dreams of the Chinese about learning from the West. It was very odd—why were the teachers always committing aggression against their pupil? The Chinese learned a good deal from the West, but they could not make it work and were never able to realize their ideals. Their repeated struggles, including such a country-wide movement as the Revolution of 1911, all ended in failure. Day by day, conditions in the country got worse, and life was made impossible. Doubts arose, increased, and deepened. World War I shook the whole globe. The Russians made the October Revolution and created the world's first socialist state. Under the leadership of Lenin and Stalin, the revolutionary energy of the great proletariat and labouring people of Russia, hitherto latent and unseen by foreigners, suddenly erupted like a volcano, and the Chinese and all mankind began to see the Russians in a new light. Then, and only then, did the Chinese enter an entirely new era in their thinking and their life. They found Marxism-Leninism, the universally applicable truth, and the face of China began to change.

It was through the Russians that the Chinese found Marxism. Before the October Revolution, the Chinese were not only ignorant of Lenin and Stalin, they did not even know of Marx and Engels. The salvoes of the October Revolution brought us Marxism-Leninism. The October Revolution helped progressives in China, as throughout the world, to adopt the proletarian world outlook as the instrument for studying a nation's destiny and considering anew their own problems. Follow the path of the Russians—that was their conclusion. In 1919, the May 4th Movement[124] took place in China. In 1921, the Communist Party of China was founded. Sun Yat-sen, in the depths of despair, came across the October Revolution and the Communist Party of China. He welcomed the October Revolution, welcomed Russian help to the Chinese and welcomed co-operation of the Communist Party of China. Then Sun Yat-sen died and Chiang Kai-shek rose to power. Over a long period of twenty-two years, Chiang Kai-shek dragged China into ever more hopeless straits. In this period, during the anti-fascist Second World War in which the Soviet Union was the main force, three big imperialist powers were knocked out, while two others were weakened. In the whole world only one big imperialist power, the United States of America, remained uninjured. But the United States faced a grave domestic crisis. It wanted to enslave the whole world; it supplied arms to help Chiang Kai-shek slaughter several million Chinese. Under the leadership of the Communist Party of China, the Chinese people, after driving out Japanese imperialism, waged the People's War of Liberation for three years and have basically won victory.

Thus Western bourgeois civilization, bourgeois democracy, and the plan for a bourgeois republic have all gone bankrupt in the eyes of the Chinese people. Bourgeois democracy has given way to people's democracy under the leadership of the working class and the bourgeois republic to the people's republic. This has made it possible to achieve socialism and communism through the people's republic, to abolish classes and enter a world of Great Harmony. . .

* * *

---

124. A political movement that emerged from student demonstrations in Beijing on May 4, 1919, protesting unfair treatment of China by the Treaty of Versailles.

Twenty-four years have passed since Sun Yat-sen's death, and the Chinese revolution, led by the Communist Party of China, has made tremendous advances both in theory and practice and has radically changed the face of China. Up to now the principal and fundamental experience the Chinese people have gained is twofold:

(1) Internally, arouse the masses of the people. That is, unite the working class, the peasantry, the urban petty bourgeoisie and the national bourgeoisie, form a domestic united front under the leadership of the working class, and advance from this to the establishment of a state which is a people's democratic dictatorship under the leadership of the working class and based on the alliance of workers and peasants.

(2) Externally, unite in a common struggle with those nations of the world which treat us as equals and unite with the peoples of all countries. That is, ally ourselves with the Soviet Union, with the People's Democracies, and with the proletariat and the broad masses of the people in all other countries, and form an international united front.

* * *

Twenty-eight years of our Party are a long period, in which we have accomplished only one thing—we have won basic victory in the revolutionary war. This calls for celebration, because it is the people's victory, because it is a victory in a country as large as China. But we still have much work to do; to use the analogy of a journey, our past work is only the first step in a long march of ten thousand *li*.[125] Remnants of the enemy have yet to be wiped out. The serious task of economic construction lies before us. We shall soon put aside some of the things we know well and be compelled to do things we don't know well. This means difficulties. The imperialists reckon that we will not be able to manage our economy; they are standing by and looking on, awaiting our failure. We must overcome difficulties; we must learn what we do not know. We must learn to do economic work from all who know how, no matter who they are. We must esteem them as teachers, learning from them respectfully and conscientiously. We must not pretend to know when we do not know. We must not put on bureaucratic airs. If we dig into a subject for several months, for a year or two, for three or five years, we shall eventually master it. At first some of the Soviet Communists also were not very good at

---

125. A traditional unit of distance, equivalent to roughly one-third mile.

handling economic matters and the imperialists awaited their failure too. But the Communist Party of the Soviet Union emerged victorious and, under the leadership of Lenin and Stalin, it learned not only how to make the revolution but also how to carry on construction. It has built a great and splendid socialist state. The Communist Party of the Soviet Union is our best teacher and we must learn from it....

SELECT BIBLIOGRAPHY

Acton, Edward, Vladimir Iu. Cherniaev, and William G. Rosenberg, eds. *Critical Companion to the Russian Revolution, 1914–1921.* London: Edward Arnold, 1997.

Arnot, Robert Page. *The Impact of the Russian Revolution in Britain.* London: Lawrence and Wishart, 1967.

Bain, Mervyn J. *From Lenin to Castro, 1917–1959: Early Encounters Between Moscow and Havana.* Lanham, MD: Lexington Books, 2013.

Barkey, Karen, and Mark von Hagen, eds. *After Empire: Multiethnic Societies and Nation-Building.* Boulder, CO: Westview Press, 1997.

Broué, Pierre. *The German Revolution, 1917–1923.* Translated by John Archer. Edited by Ian Birchall and Brian Pearce. With an Introduction by Eric D. Weitz. Chicago: Haymarket Books, 2006.

Brown, Archie. *The Rise and Fall of Communism.* New York: HarperCollins, 2009.

Buck, Tim. *Canada and the Russian Revolution: The Impact of the World's First Socialist Revolution on Labor and Politics in Canada.* Toronto: Progress Books, 1967.

Burbank, Jane and Frederick Cooper. *Empires in World History: Power and Politics of Difference.* Princeton, NJ: Princeton University Press, 2011.

Carew, Joy Gleason. *Blacks, Reds, and Russians: Sojourners in Search of the Soviet Promise.* New Brunswick, NJ: Rutgers University Press, 2008.

Carley, Michael Jabara. *Silent Conflict: A Hidden History of Early Soviet-Western Relations.* Lanham, MD: Rowman & Littlefield, 2014.

Carr, Edward H. *A History of Soviet Russia.* New York: Macmillan, 1950–1978.

Caute, David. *Communism and the French Intellectuals, 1914–1960.* New York: Macmillan, 1964.

Cliff, Tony. *Lenin: The Bolsheviks and the World Revolution.* London: Pluto Press, 1979.

Davidson, Apollon, et al., eds. *South Africa and the Communist International: A Documentary History.* 2 vols. London and Portland, OR: Frank Cass, 2003.

Debo, Richard K. *Survival and Consolidation: The Foreign Policy of Soviet Russia, 1918–1921*. Montreal and Kingston: McGill-Queen's University Press, 1992.

D'Encausse, Helene. *The Great Challenge: Nationalities and the Bolshevik State, 1917–1930*. New York: Holmes and Meier, 1992.

Dukes, Paul. *October and the World: Perspectives on the Russian Revolution*. New York: St. Martin's Press, 1979.

Dukes, Paul. *World Order in History: Russia and the West*. London and New York: Routledge, 1996.

Duncan, Peter J. S. *Russian Messianism: Third Rome, Revolution, Communism, and After*. London: Routledge, 2000.

Fischer, Louis. *The Soviets in World Affairs: A History of the Relations Between the Soviet Union and the Rest of the World, 1917–1929*. 2d ed. Princeton: Princeton University Press, 1951.

Foner, Philip Sheldon. *The Bolshevik Revolution: Its Impact on American Radicals, Liberals and Labor*. New York: International Publishers, 1967.

Frame, Murray. *The Russian Revolution 1905–1921: A Bibliographic Guide to Works in English*. Westport, CT: Greenwood Press, 1995.

Goldstone, Jack. *Revolutions: A Very Short Introduction*. Oxford and New York: Oxford University Press, 2014.

Gorodetsky, Gabriel, ed. *Soviet Foreign Policy, 1917–1991: A Retrospective*. London and Portland, OR: Frank Cass, 1994.

Haigh, R. H., D. S. Morris, and A. R. Peters. *Soviet Foreign Policy, The League of Nations and Europe, 1917–1939*. Totowa, NJ: Barnes & Noble Books, 1986.

Hallas, Duncan. *The Comintern*. Chicago: Haymarket Books, 2008.

Harding, Neil. *Leninism*. Durham, NC: Duke University Press, 1996.

Hobsbawm, Eric. *Age of Extremes: The Short Twentieth Century, 1914–1991*. New York: Viking Penguin, 1994.

Holquist, Peter. *Making War, Forging Revolution: Russia's Continuum of Crisis, 1914–1921*. Cambridge, MA: Harvard University Press, 2002.

Jackson, George, and Robert James Devlin, eds. *Dictionary of the Russian Revolution*. New York: Greenwood Press, 1989.

Jacobson, Jon. *When the Soviet Union Entered World Politics*. Berkeley: University of California Press, 1994.

Janos, Andrew C., and William Slottman, eds. *Revolution in Perspective: Essays on the Hungarian Soviet Republic of 1919*. Berkeley, CA: University of California Press, 1971.

Katz, Mark N., ed. *Revolution: International Dimensions.* Washington, DC: CQ Press, 2001.

Klehr, Harvey. *The Soviet World of American Communism.* New Haven: Yale University Press, 1998.

Krejčií, Jaroslav, and Anna Krejčováá. *Great Revolutions Compared: The Outline of a Theory.* New York: Harvester Wheatsheaf, 1994.

Lazic, Branco. *Biographical Dictionary of the Comintern.* Stanford: Hoover Institution Press, 1986.

Levine, Alan J. *The Soviet Union, the Communist Movement, and the World: Prelude to the Cold War, 1917–1941.* New York: Praeger, 1990.

Malia, Martin E. *History's Locomotives: Revolutions and the Making of the Modern World.* Edited by Terence Emmons. New Haven: Yale University Press, 2006.

Marks, Steven G. *How Russia Shaped the Modern World.* Princeton: Princeton University Press, 2004.

Moore, Barrington. *Dictatorship and Democracy: Lord and Peasant in the Making of the Modern World.* Boston: Beacon Press, 1966.

Neilson, K. *Britain, Soviet Russia, and the Collapse of the Versailles Order, 1919–1939.* Cambridge and New York: Cambridge University Press, 2006.

Pantsov, Alexander. *The Bolsheviks and the Chinese Revolution, 1919–1927.* Honolulu: University of Hawaii Press, 2000.

Pipes, Richard. *Communism: A History.* New York: Modern Library, 2001.

Pons, Silvio. *The Global Revolution: A History of International Communism, 1917–1991.* Translated by Allen Cameron. Oxford: Oxford University Press, 2014.

Priestland, David. *The Red Flag: Communism and the Making of the Modern World.* London: Allen Lane, 2009.

Read, Anthony. *The World on Fire: 1919 and the Battle with Bolshevism.* New York: W. W. Norton & Company, 2008.

Richards, Michael D. *Revolutions in World History.* London and New York: Routledge, 2004.

Ridell, John. *To See the Dawn: Baku, 1920, First Congress of the Peoples of the East.* New York: Pathfinder Press, 1993.

Sanderson, Stephen K. *Revolutions: A Worldwide Introduction to Social and Political Change.* Boulder, CO and London: Paradigm, 2005.

Service, Robert. *Comrades! A History of World Communism.* Cambridge, MA: Harvard University Press, 2007.

Shakibi, Zhand. *Revolutions and the Collapse of Monarchy: Human Agency and the Making of Revolution in France, Russia, and Iran*. London and New York: I. B. Taurus, 2007.

Skocpol, Theda. *States and Social Revolutions: A Comparative Analysis of France, Russia, and China*. Cambridge and New York: Cambridge University Press, 1979.

Smele, Jonathan D. *Historical Dictionary of the Russian Civil Wars, 1916–1926*. Lanham, MD: Rowman & Littlefield, 2015.

Smele, Jonathan D. *The Russian Revolution and Civil War, 1917–1921: An Annotated Bibliography*. London and New York: Continuum, 2003.

Smith, S. A. *The Russian Revolution: A Very Short Introduction*. Oxford and New York: Oxford University Press, 2002.

Sondhaus, Lawrence. *World War I: The Global Revolution*. Cambridge and New York: Cambridge University Press, 2011

Spenser, Daniel. *The Impossible Triangle: Mexico, Soviet Russia, and the United States in the 1920s*. Durham, NC: Duke University Press, 1999.

Steiner, Zara. *The Lights That Failed: European International History, 1919–1933*. Oxford and New York: Oxford University Press, 2005.

Stone, Bailey. *The Anatomy of Revolution Revisited: A Comparative Analysis of England, France, and Russia*. Cambridge and New York: Cambridge University Press, 2014.

Suny, Ronald Grigor. *The Revenge of the Past: Nationalism, Revolution, and the Collapse of the Soviet Union*. Stanford: Stanford University Press, 2004.

Swain, Geoffrey. *Trotsky and the Russian Revolution*. London and New York: Routledge, 2014.

Toynbee, Arnold Joseph. *The Impact of the Russian Revolution, 1917–1967: The Influence of Bolshevism on the World Outside Russia*. London and New York: Oxford University Press, 1967.

Ulam, Adam. *Expansion and Coexistence: Soviet Foreign Policy, 1917–73*. New York: Praeger, 1974.

Uldricks, Teddy J. *Diplomacy and Ideology: The Origins of Soviet Foreign Relations, 1917–1930*. London and Beverly Hills: SAGE Publications, 1979.

Vourkoutiotis, Vasilis. *Making Common Cause: German-Soviet Secret Relations, 1919–22*. Basingstoke and New York: Palgrave Macmillan, 2007.

Wade, Rex. *Documents of Soviet History*. Vol 3: *Lenin's Heirs*. Gulf Breeze, FL: Academic International Pr., 1995.

Wade, Rex A. *The Russian Revolution, 1917*. 3d Edition. Cambridge: Cambridge University Press, 2017.

Weiner Amir. *Making Sense of War: The Second World War and the Fate of the Bolshevik Revolution*. Princeton and Oxford: Princeton University Press, 2001.

Young, Glennys. *The Communist Experience in the Twentieth Century: A Global History through Sources*. Oxford and New York: Oxford University Press, 2011.

INDEX